River Musings

To Pat and Jan
Good neighbors and good friends
Peace!
Vivian R. Pryce
9/23/03

River Musings

Vivian R. Pyke

iUniverse, Inc.
New York Lincoln Shanghai

River Musings

iUniverse, Inc.

For information address:
iUniverse, Inc.
2021 Pine Lake Road, Suite 100
Lincoln, NE 68512
www.iuniverse.com

ISBN: 0-595-29242-9

Printed in the United States of America

To Charles who gave me the space

To Gene who showed me the way

Contents

1999

2000

ACKNOWLEDGEMENTS

I wish to express my deep appreciation to members of my Sanibel-Captiva Writers' Group, who lovingly critiqued the essays in this book. With words of encouragement, and "tongue in cheek," they frequently hacked away at the final sentence of most of my pieces, thereby making them stronger. I especially thank Betty Anholt, Eleanor and Don Brown, Carol Ehrlich, Dick Jacker, Sallie Rich, Ruth Iyengar, Judy Maurer, Maria Faraone, Cecie Munkenbeck, Steve Oberbeck, Michael Derechin, Tom Simmons, Di Saggau, Joan Grindley and Summer Moon Bear for their enthusiasm and support.

I'm thankful to David Brown for introducing me to the computer, and to Don Maurer, who helped me immeasurably to upgrade my skills. Without them the task of writing this book would have been tedious.

I wish to thank Jeanne Snow, editor of the <u>Thousand</u> <u>Island</u> <u>Sun</u> and members of the staff for the opportunity to share, through my weekly column, these <u>River</u> <u>Musings</u> with the Sun's readers throughout northern New York and beyond.

Introduction

As a year-round islander, I live in the best of two worlds, and write about both of them. The short essays contained in this book were inspired by my island life, and first appeared in the Thousand Island Sun, a weekly newspaper published in Alexandria Bay, New York.

I grew up in a land-locked community in Vermont. With infrequent visits to a nearby lake, my water-loving spirit felt incomplete—lacking in some unknown avenue for expression. When my husband first introduced me to Wellesley Island in the middle of the St. Lawrence River, something deep inside me suddenly resonated. I felt a strong sense of coming home. Isolation and the magnificent river just outside my front door gave me the distance I needed to allow my spirit to roam the world of wonder and imagination. I have been relishing and writing ever since.

I spend the spring, summer and fall months on the river. After crossing the high suspension toll bridge over the American channel, I take a meandering drive through the state park and arrive at a point of land called Grand View Park. There, among a cluster of about twenty-five, sits our cottage, the "Aquarium," so named because we filled it with Pykes.

Wellesley is approximately ten miles long and five miles wide, and contains no large communities or major shopping facilities. Thousand Island Park, a small settlement in existence since before the turn of the twentieth century, has a corner convenience store. Its narrow roads are lined with Victorian cottages, some of which are on the National Registry of historic homes. The recently restored Pavilion on the river is also on the Registry. A great place to go to by boat, it's fun to dock there and walk the short distance to "The Guzzle," an old-fashioned ice cream parlor adjacent to the convenience store, for a treat on a hot summer day.

Wellesley Island provides a link between the United States and Canada. Summer traffic is substantial, but side roads are quiet. At Grand View our grandchildren ride bikes and play ball on the gravel road between the cottages.

Without street lights I can lie on my dock in the evening and look up at a sky studded with millions of stars, watch a moon rise across the water, and wonder what it's really like up there.

When campers in the state park leave after Labor Day, the island becomes my private estate and I can wander about, scuffling through fallen leaves, uninterrupted by human sounds. If I am quiet, I may see a few deer grazing in the now-empty fields that separate the campsites. I stay at my northern island until the air becomes crisp, the leaves have fallen and snow threatens.

Just before gray November descends, I head south to Sanibel, my other island home, on the west coast of Florida. To cross to this island I must pass through a toll booth and over a causeway with a drawbridge and two other bridges.

Though my two islands are similar in size, they are quite different in other ways. Sanibel has a substantial permanent community with many shops and restaurants, including two grocery stores. During the busy winter tourist season, traffic on the main road of the island is bumper to bumper. However, the side streets are quiet and rural in atmosphere. Instead of worrying about acorns denting the top of my car, I must watch out for coconuts falling on my head. I don't see deer, but I watch ibis, egrets, wood storks and blue herons scouting for food along the shore of the lake outside my window. It is not unusual to see an alligator cruising down the middle of the lake. The Gulf of Mexico is about a mile from my home. On the beach I can see shore birds and watch dolphins as they fish for breakfast.

Each of my islands offers me space for quiet reflection, and a chance to view a starry sky away from bright lights and heavy traffic. And there is always the variety and stimulation, which provides material for the short essays contained in this book.

I feel richly blessed.

1997

Give me a spark o' nature's fire,
That's a' the learning I desire.

Robert Burns

A Walk In The Rain

Six a.m. Rain fell in a fine mist. Fog shrouded the becalmed and silent river in its gentle flow toward the distant sea. No wind rustled the delicate half-formed leaves on the trees. I looked at the thermometer. Fifty degrees. A weighty decision. Should I go out for my morning walk?

Standing on my favorite rocky outcropping at the edge of the river, surrounded by the fog, I feel as though I'm the only person in this whole world. Here, there is no sound of traffic, human voices, or anything else to remind me that others are nearby. My aloneness fills me with delight.

Except for the tops of a few pine trees towering above the pearly fog, the islands across the way are hidden from my view. I feel a sense of mystery in all this whiteness, and catch my breath at such beauty.

But where does beauty lie? A half-mile back on the road by the boat ramp, several fishermen hunker around their boats, cursing the weather that keeps them bound to the shore. They watch the same scene as I.

I continue to walk, listening to the songs of the birds—red-wing blackbirds, robins, Baltimore orioles, meadow larks, and an occasional screech of a blue jay. They seem to sing for the pure joy of being alive.

Rounding a bend in the road, I come upon a huge turtle lumbering his way across the road. His shell is more than a foot across at its widest part. Neck extended, legs stretched to their fullest length, he staggers as he walks. Halfway across the road he notices me and warily slumps down onto the bottom of his shell, withdraws his head part-way, and watches me with beady eyes. I stand and watch him, noticing the thick leathery folds of his neck pulsating rhythmically as he breathes. After a brief stand-off, I continue on my way. Looking back, I note that he takes no chances. He remains watchful and unmoving.

Ahead of me two deer have caught my scent and stop grazing. They are on opposite sides of the road, and are clearly nervous. I stop to see what they will do. One watches me with limpid brown eyes, ears and nose twitching. She appears more curious than afraid. The other swishes her tail and stomps her foot. She does not like being separated from her companion. Finally, she can no longer stand the threat, and bounds off into the woods, leaving her partner to fend for herself. I feel privileged to see those lovely creatures at such close range.

Heading for home and a warm breakfast, I notice many different shades of green in the newly emerging springtime—pale green leaves, blue-green low-growing ground cover, chartreuse moss cling to wet rocks. Creator has spread a magnificent visual banquet for my feasting.

Beauty lies not in a thing or a place, but rather, in my personal response to those things I choose to observe in my wanderings. I'm glad I came.

Trees

This morning I walked through the gothic arch of maple trees at Grand View. I noticed how old and tired they look. Some have already fallen prey to wind, weather, disease and decay. They leave gaping holes and ragged stumps to remind me of their more stately days. Their trunks lay in a crumbling heap amid the ferns on the forest floor.

Other trees seem to be hanging onto their final days by sheer will power. Soon, they too will succumb to the ravages of time and weather. I felt sad. My green canopy is slowly disappearing.

I stood in the middle of the road, in the midst of all this decay, and pondered the ways of nature. The old trees have come to the end of their time. Then I noticed that in the empty spaces right beside the ancient ones, new life has sprung up. Small saplings are growing strong and straight beneath the sheltering arms of the "old folks."

Summer has arrived, and with it, rebirth. A new generation is being formed. Once more nature proves that life is eternal. Faith and hope are continually being acted out in these woods so close to my home.

River Walk

This morning as I walked in the woods, I saw a mother and three baby raccoons, heard the raucous screech of a noisy crow, got a friendly nod from a giant oak, and experienced a hint of eternity.

Along the road I stopped for a momentary exchange with an early morning jogger and an acorn thumped on my head. Farther on, deeper into the woods, I became aware of the silent scrutiny of a wary doe. I stopped to reassure her that I would not invade her territory for long, and would do her no harm. I felt a deep sense of peace and tranquility.

In a clearing where I could see the river, I counted twenty gliding geese on the surface of the water and watched a mama duck and six ducklings swimming among the weeds along the shore. I sniffed a faint waft of smoke from a distant campfire, and felt at one with nature.

Back behind the state park campsites I heard frogs cheeping in the beaver pond, and saw squirrels scampering among the trees. Through the canopy of trees I watched an eagle soaring high in the sky.

What a marvelous banquet! All my senses were nourished and I felt a strong sensation of pure aliveness.

Night

The river is a great mirror—marked only by clumps of scattered islands. The sky and river are the same steel gray.

The trees stand silent. Their new leaves hang limp.

A lone bird flies past my window—his last flight before bedding down for the night.

My heart slows its beat, as if to match the serenity of the scene before me. A deep silence settles over me. I am relaxed, but alert to the slightest movement or the faintest sound. At the moment there is neither.

Night creeps in slowly and gently. Shadows deepen. The islands are still sharply outlined against the darkening sky, but soon they will disappear—become one with the black of late night.

No moon shines across the water tonight. The sky is completely overcast.

Now I see blinking lights on the channel markers across the way—red, green. They were not there a moment ago. The scene appears frozen in stillness. Yet there is movement, almost imperceptible. Beneath the placid surface, the river continues its flow toward the far-away sea.

My soul rests peacefully.

The Oak Tree

I walk past the old oak tree that stands by the road at the top of a hill in the Wellesley Island state park. This tree is imposing, with a diameter of about four feet. I dare say it has been standing here for well over two hundred years. Something makes me turn back, stand in front of it and look up at its broad expanse of branches. Do I only imagine that it smiles at me?

I begin to hear the leaves whisper in the light breeze. Today they could speak quietly. Other days they have to shout above the noise of the raging wind and crashing waves. I listen intently as they speak to me of patience and fortitude, of longevity, and also of impermanence. This tree, like all other living things, had a beginning, a mid-life, and now, perhaps, is approaching an ending. I notice it is not as full as I remember it just a few years ago. It grows tired, though it still serves me lovingly with grace and beauty, offering protective shade from the sun's rays, shelter from rain, and the assurance of a benevolent Presence more powerful than both of us.

This tree, if allowed to complete its life cycle naturally, will not end in nothingness. It will one day just heave a loud sigh and fall over in a great heap, or perhaps be violently rent, its branches tossed about in the midst of a fierce storm, finally, to lie quietly rotting. Woodpeckers will drill holes in its massive trunk searching for food. Squirrels will come and build nests in the holes. It will slowly turn to humus. One day an acorn will fall from a neighboring tree, find a nurturing environment, sprout, and grow. New life will begin. My oak tree lives again!

History

A gray mist hangs heavy over the old red barn by the side of the road, shrouding it in mystery.

I wonder who built that barn. It must have served some useful purpose when it was new, but it stands empty now, slowly deteriorating in its lonely abandonment.

As I travel down the highway, I notice more abandoned buildings, reminders of a long-ago more prosperous time. If they could talk, I wonder what stories they would tell. Would it be important for me to hear their tales? Could I benefit from their history?

I think about old people languishing in nursing homes, many of whom are discarded, alone, rejected by the mainstream of society. They, too, have stories to tell. Can they also teach me something valuable about how to weave the fabric of my own life?

I have read that there is a universal form of intelligence encased in every single cell of all life-forms which is interconnected. Whatever experience occurs in the life of one cell can be transmitted to other cells anywhere in the world, even among those not directly connected to the original organism. If this is so, then when one old person is consigned to the back hallways of life, perhaps in some small way my own life is diminished. Can I live to the fullest of my ability while I sit by and let someone else shrink into nothingness from sheer neglect?

Community

After a week of absence, I took the time today to walk in the woods. Following a deer trail, I wound my way deep into the forest. The silence was complete. Nothing moved. As I opened myself up to the stillness, I became aware of a profound sense of aliveness, and a wonderful demonstration of community in its purest form.

As I looked about, I realized that every element of this forest works in perfect cooperation with every other element. Although the trees stand quite close together, they have left enough space between them for each one to grow according to its will. The branches spread out and intermingle at the top in a thick canopy, with just enough openness for light to shine through to nurture the grasses and ground cover below. There are oak trees that grow acorns to provide food at the right time of year for squirrels to gather and store for the winter months. Berries on some of the bushes offer the deer a tasty dessert to top off their diet of grass and young sprouts.

I saw no crowding, hoarding, or fighting for the best position—only accommodation and harmony as far as the eye could travel.

Millions of children in this country grow up in a concrete jungle, with never an opportunity to observe, on a regular basis, nature close at hand. No wonder we have a hard time teaching them the values of community. Mother nature is, by far, the best teacher.

I Am A Rock

As I walked in the woods one day, I wandered into a ravine just large enough for two campsites. It is a favorite spot I can't visit in the summer because campers are there. But this was an early spring day before the State Park was open to the public, and I had it all to myself. I sat on a picnic table and looked up at the rocky hillside that skirted the edge of the ravine. On the face of the rock I saw the roots of a large oak tree stretching down the side like a giant hand with knobby fingers, holding onto the rock for dear life. A story began to unfold in my head:

There is a rock—a big, strong, silent old rock. Once, a long time ago, a tiny oak seed dropped onto the top of this rock. It settled there in companionable silence, taking its sustenance from the adjacent soil. Soon it grew into a young tree and needed more. It began to reach out to the rock for support. Its roots grew around the rock, reaching, grabbing, squeezing, with growing tentacles surrounding the rock, becoming ever more dependent on the rock for support. The rock stood silent, unmoving, continuing to be what it really is—a rock. The rock allowed the tree to do its own thing, but would not be changed.

Gradually, the tree stretched and grew until its roots reached the ground under and around the rock. There it could find more nourishment, the kind that would sustain it. The rock stood strong, accepting the tree's presence, allowing it to be, but also maintaining its own identity.

I am a rock!

The Beaver Pond

I walked in the woods this morning. The sky was overcast; fog drifted across the river; mist rose from the surface of the beaver pond. Frogs croaked at each other across the dead tree trunks and small branches that cluttered the pond. I stopped to admire a pair of mallard ducks snoozing on a limb that lay just above the surface of the water. While I stood there, a little chipmunk ran right across my foot. In that moment I felt a strong sense of belonging, as if I were an integral part of the forest scene, no longer an objective observer.

If this is so, then I must behave as the forest creatures do. I can take what I need from the earth, but I must give back something that will help to maintain a balance and continue the great cycle of growth and change.

The beaver cuts down huge trees to build his dam, which in turn floods the land and kills all the undergrowth. At first glance, this seems very destructive. Upon closer observation, I see that this new pond provides a home for myriad small swimming creatures, and a wonderful place for ducks to nest and raise their families. The cycle of life continues.

I can learn to live in harmony with my environment. Native Americans lived in peaceful co-existence with their surroundings for hundreds of years before my ancestors arrived in this land. They took only what they needed to live comfortably, and did not pollute the land, air and water with their waste.

Will I, before it is too late, agree to do the same?

Meditation

After weeks of warm, sunny weather and empty promises of much-needed rain, the real thing finally happened. The rain pelts down relentlessly, and I am alone in a delicious, deliberate slowdown.

The river is still, silent and abandoned—not a boat in sight. Even the islands are remote in their almost nonexistence.

My spirit has withdrawn from the real world to a place of peaceful meditation. Or is it the other way around? Perhaps the place where my soul resides is the real part, and the rest of life is make-believe; cluttered with trivia, imagined importance and seemingly urgent activities.

The river, in her disregard for the elements, man-made encumbrances such as docks and artificial shorelines, even life itself, teaches me about what is important and what is real. She reminds me that she makes her own rules. I need her life-giving support in order to survive. My own body is made up of mostly water.

But this river also reminds me that if I disobey her rules she will take my life away, swallow me into her depths, only to spew me out days or even weeks later. She is unforgiving!

I have a great deal of love and respect for this mighty St. Lawrence River. If I learn her ways, give her the freedom she needs to flow naturally northward to the sea, and cease polluting her waters with my waste, she will reward me with pure water for drinking, clear water for swimming, abundant fishing, and magnificent reflections of sky, trees, clouds and multi-colored sunsets unsurpassed anywhere in the land.

Fog

The fog just rolled in, obscuring my world, and for a little while it seems as if I am all alone in a fantasy land. No one is around.

A few moments ago, I could see the trees in my yard, and the river out front—beyond, more trees, and houses across the river. Further on, a road, more houses, another river. And even beyond that, other streets, and houses, bodies of water, more towns, cities, countries—the whole world. If I keep going, I know I will come back to my starting point. How do I know that? Some one told me the earth is round; I also read it in a book. But, best of all, I can see it for myself. If I sit at the water's edge and look out to the horizon, the sun will not suddenly show all of itself to me; it will come up bit by bit from around the other side of the curve in the earth.

However, right now, at this moment, there is nothing—no sun, moon, stars; no countries, cities, rivers or persons. I only see white fog, so thick I can taste it, feel it on my skin. For a little while, I experience the nothingness—complete isolation.

I am not frightened by this nothingness, because, though it seems real to me at this moment, it is not. In truth, the world out there still exists, and the people in it, too.

This causes me to ponder the nature of reality, and to ask the question, "What is truth?" So often I think I know something—I am right, therefore it is the truth. But someone else might know the same thing and be absolutely sure it is wrong. A different truth begins to emerge. Who is right? What is truth? Which is real?

I begin to see, in the midst of all this whiteness and nothingness, that reality and truth are relative. What seems real to me may be unreal to you. What is my truth may not be yours. When I stick to my truth, live my life according to my reality, I always know what is right for me, and it leaves me in peace. When I acknowledge your right to do the same, I feel good about you.

The fog creeps away as silently as it came, and the world takes on its familiar perspective. I am here and you are there, and sometimes we touch.

Riverfront Musings

The last day of August. Summer is ending. I sit on the deck by the water, basking in sunlight, cooled by a gentle breeze.

My son-in-law brought me a piece of driftwood, all gnarled, knotted and twisted into a gnome-like shape, really quite beautiful. When it is bleached, it will look nice on my deck table. Mother Nature never sleeps, and creates beauty from the most mundane things.

I could learn from that.

A big sailboat came gliding around the point at Grand View, tacking into the wind. It changed course right in front of me. Briefly, the sails flapped in disarray, but with a slight adjustment, they caught the wind again, and off went the boat.

Sails can take me far, but they need a strong hand to set them on the right path. If I don't man the ropes, I will go nowhere.

Something to remember.

The over-hanging branch provides me with shade from the sun. But the tree it is a part of leans precariously over my deck. The tree man says it is secure right now, but one day it will need to be removed. How do I strike a balance between shade and safety?

Always there is a need for balance. Too much of anything overwhelms me. An over-long vacation is no longer a vacation. Too much company wears me out. Long exposure to the sun burns my skin. Continuous introspection takes me away from using what I have learned from all my musing.

I will do well to learn from that.

Richly Blessed

The days grow short, the leaves are turning, morning dew is heavy, and a chill wind whips across the river, reminding me that summer is ending. Before long, my husband and I will expend considerable amounts of energy lugging wood to feed the hungry fire we will need to keep us warm. The air in late September turns crisp and clear. Though fresh and invigorating, it generally does not lend itself to lazy lingering.

In just a few weeks we will pack up to head south. Our winter home is on a little lake on Sanibel Island in Florida. The trip south will take us from the fall of New York and Pennsylvania, through the Virginias, the Carolinas where fall is just beginning, to the late summer of Georgia, and finally to southern Florida where the snows of winter never grace the land.

In the first days after my arrival, I will rest, late in the day, on my porch and reflect on the ways of nature. There, the gentle breezes stir. The trees across the lake glow in the day's waning light as if touched by King Midas. Sounds of civilization echo in the distance, but all will be calm and serene where I sit.

Two worlds—each with its own pull on my soul at different times of the year. On the surface they appear quite different, but they both offer me the same thing—the opportunity to live close to natural surroundings, the chance to view a starry sky unbroken by bright lights, to quietly observe wildlife at close range, and to ponder the awesome wonder of the universe.

The transition from one world to the other leaves me disoriented for a little while—until I connect with something unique to this part of my life, and I once again experience a sense of belonging.

1998

Peace comes within the souls of men
When they realize their oneness with the universe.

Black Elk

Two Worlds

The winter of cold winds, icy roads, snow piled high in the driveway, heavy coats and boots to keep feet warm and dry has passed while here on Sanibel I have enjoyed shorts and sleeveless tops, sandals and a daily swim in the pool. When I was young I loved the cold crisp days of winter with sun sparkling on a snowy landscape. At this point in my life it is nice to remember without having to experience it.

Now, late in April, it is time to think about our annual migration to the north country where family and other friends await our arrival. In the meantime:

The early morning sun casts an ethereal glow on the lake outside my window. Ibis, egrets and little blue herons poke for their breakfast along the shore.

This morning I watched a six-foot alligator glide by. He made only a small ripple on the still water and did not disturb the birds. They, in turn, ignored him.

It was a quiet, peaceful way to start my day. I felt ready for whatever the day might bring.

Soon, I will leave this place, and travel north to spend the summer months on my beloved St. Lawrence River. When I look out my window there, I see water in a very different setting. The wide expanse of river, dotted with islands, has a perceptible current as it threads its way to the sea. It is rarely calm. In the slightest breeze, ripples break the blue wash of water as it gently slaps against the shore. Even on a quiet day gulls landing on the water bounce.

Some days the river comes crashing down from the lake beyond like a raging bull bent on disrupting everything in its path. I retreat from its shore with respect for its awesome power—but it is invigorating to watch.

Two worlds—each with its own special charm, each nurturing my spirit.

Ice Storm Thoughts

I'm almost afraid to return to my river island. I am told it was not the wind alone that did the damage, but the relentless freezing rain. It built up several inches of ice on trees already burdened by the ravages of time. Once they were mighty oaks, now their tops and branches are broken and dangling, vulnerable to any strong wind. I weep for the loss. My woods will never be the same.

But wait—is that not true for all of life? Change is inevitable, however it might come about. If I can step back and look at the larger picture, I will see some purpose in everything that happens. Nature can wreak havoc. She also heals.

Those trees had a magnificent life, but it is coming to an end. For several years the trees have been falling, one by one, in stormy weather and on quiet days alike. Perhaps it is time for them to depart to make way for the new saplings that even now are sprouting.

I'm just sad that this change has happened so quickly and in such a devastating manner. I know I will not live long enough to see the new trees towering almost a hundred feet in the air as their parents have for all the years I have known them.

As in everything else in life, I can continue to mourn the loss of the old, or adjust and accept the new.

Choices

"Into every life a little rain must fall." "The best laid plans—." Cliches which had little meaning for me until April eighteen of this year when I fell off my bicycle and suffered a break in my ankle. Surgery was required to secure it. My doctor said, "No weight bearing for eight weeks."

My orderly world was suddenly turned upside down. Plans to return to my Wellesley Island home were now put on hold. I would not get there in time to watch the new leaves unfold on the trees, the grass grow green and the trillium poke through the undergrowth in the woods.

But wait. All is not lost. Memory and imagination have come to my rescue. I have only to close my eyes, quiet my mind and engage in some mental imagery.

I can clearly see through the pale green leaves on the trees the white heads of trillium emerging from their long winter's sleep. The ferns are unfurling in graceful, feathery fronds. I hear blue jays screeching in the distance. As I stand at the edge of the woods, I can smell the fresh dampness of new life all around me. The earth is waking up, reassuring me of the eternal nature of all of life.

Memory is a marvelous gift. Imagination is remembering what once was, or what could be. I will use both to sustain me in the weeks to come.

Meanwhile, here on my Sanibel Island the days grow hot and humid. Fish jump in the lake outside my window. Butterflies flit, and osprey whistle over-head. A lone alligator crawls up the bank across the lake to bask in the afternoon sun.

Always there are choices. I can weep for the feast that eludes me, or enjoy the banquet laid out before me. I have made my choice.

Homecoming

Finally, after weeks of waiting for my ankle to heal, on June sixth we crossed the majestic Thousand Island Bridge onto Wellesley Island. I became silent—almost holding my breath, trying to prepare myself for what I had been told awaited me at Grand View.

The grass was green, the trees and bushes were fully leafed out, softening the bruised and tortured landscape. I grew hopeful—maybe my children were exaggerating. Of course a few trees fell. We always lose some in a storm. Perhaps a few more this time, but nothing that we couldn't absorb in the normal course of events.

As we drove through the State Park I could see that the grounds crew had been busy cleaning up the remains of broken and fallen trees. We rounded the final bend in the park, and there stood my precious giant oak, nearly naked, with several major limbs missing, tenaciously hanging onto what remains of its long and illustrious life. I wept for its loss.

We approached the gravel road leading into Grand View. My stomach turned over; I became totally disoriented with shock and dismay. I knew we were on the right road, but could find nothing that even slightly resembled a familiar landmark. Gone was the cathedral-like canopy of trees which had welcomed me to my island home for more than fifty years. In its place were piles of dried branches on either side of the road, rising higher than the top of the car. Broken tree-trunks stood like giant spears, jagged and leafless. The forest floor was strewn with fallen trees and limbs.

Tears of unbearable grief rolled down my cheeks as I tried to absorb the transformation. In one agonizing moment I knew that my familiar landscape was changed forever. I would never again ride beneath that magnificent canopy of green.

But faith and hope remain tenacious. New young saplings are already taking advantage of the increased amount of sunlight, sprouting sturdy branches and an abundance of shiny green leaves. Almost hidden beneath the tangle of dead branches, ferns struggle upward through whatever space they can find. Perhaps one day my grandchildren will again travel beneath a new canopy of trees.

Mother Nature is working diligently to heal the earth's scars. It is up to me, with the help of Creator, to heal my spirit.

Possessing

While walking in the park one morning, I noticed that all the birch trees in the camping area are either dead or dying. A substantial part of their bark was stripped, probably by someone bent on possessing some of the beauty that makes these trees unique. But this same bark had another more vital function; it protected the part of the tree that carried life-giving fluids to the branches and leaves. Without that protection the trees became vulnerable to disease, and have died, their beauty lost to all who come to enjoy. I feel cheated.

I thought about "possessing" when I remembered seeing the trillium in the woods last spring, waving their white heads in the gentle breeze. I could pick those flowers and place them in a vase to decorate my table for a few days, or I could leave them in their natural setting for everyone to enjoy, and, like the daffodils in my garden, they would last for more than two weeks.

I ponder this grasping need when I see people who appear determined to possess a spouse or a child, squelching his or her every attempt to relate to others in a normal, healthy and life-giving way.

In every instance the "possessed" is diminished, depleted, and ultimately destroyed.

I can remember that the next time I am tempted to "possess."

Voices

I sit on a rock in the woods. The wind is still—so I can hear other voices. I listen to the early morning symphony of bird songs speaking to me of boundless joy, of celebration and faith in the present moment. Today is enough. Tomorrow does not exist.

The slanting rays of the sun filter through the trees and warms a spot on my back. I feel an assurance of eternal love.

The Standing People, a Native American expression for trees, whisper to me of peace, fortitude and continuity. In the midst of such pristine beauty, my childhood view of God comes to mind and sounds a discordant note. I recall my youthful picture of an ancient man on a throne in a white robe, a kind of super-human who sits in judgement of all mortals, meting out rewards for good deeds, and punishment for wrong-doing. Back then I learned of "God's love," but it seemed that I would have to earn it by being good—and I wasn't sure whose definition of "good" He would accept.

This picture came from my child's imagination, from admonitions of my parents, thunderous sermons from the church pulpit, and lessons from well-meaning Sunday school teachers. So ingrained was this image that I have had a hard time letting it go—until recent years when I have taken the time to sit in the woods and hear with my inner ear the message of Creation so magnificent, so universal, so true no words can adequately describe it. This truth must be experienced.

I now know I am an integral part of the divine plan, that love is forever and unconditional, and that I have been created with the gift of freedom—to choose to live in concert with the Standing People, the birds and animals, the universe and other human beings, or behave in ways that will alienate me from my self and all other beings. To take what I need for sustenance, and to give back so others might also live is to recognize and accept this divine plan.

The message this morning is so loud and clear, I wonder that I don't hear it more often.

Waves

I stand on the ocean beach and watch the waves crash onto the shore. I notice they are all different. Some build fast to a high point and then crash with a mighty roar. They seem to expend their energy quickly, and they don't run very far.

Other waves come in from afar, rising gently to a rounded mountain and then just tumble over in a long roll on the sand.

Some waves wait until the last minute to rise up and then fall over with a quick smash. They don't make very much noise, but they spill many shell fragments onto the shore.

Sometimes I think a wave is coming close and I quickly retreat, only to find that it suddenly turns sideways and runs off down the beach.

I'm so busy watching these waves that I fail to notice the approach of a long, slow roller that doesn't break or make any noise at all. The next thing I know, I am standing ankle-deep in water.

Waves are like people. Though they come from a common source, they are unique in the way they express themselves.

A Call To Worship

Last night as the sun set orange in the western sky, I heard a loon call across the water. I heard a distant answering call. I don't know what they were saying to each other, but my spirit responded to that sound with a deep sense of quietude. Like the workers in the field in Millet's painting, The Angelus, who drop their sheaves of wheat and bow their heads in prayer at the sound of the bells tolling the hour of prayer, I stopped what I was doing and drifted into another realm...

Years ago, on a Sunday morning in a little town in Switzerland, my friend Dawn and I were strolling down the main street when we heard the tolling of heavenly-sounding bells. Dawn was sure they were church bells. I wanted to believe that—they were so clear and melodious in the crisp, cool air. But something prodded me to follow the sound to its source.

We walked past a line of tiny shops to the end of the street and were suddenly out in the country looking up the steep hills. There on a grassy hillside we discovered our "church bells" hanging from the necks of cows peacefully grazing in the field. With each bob of their heads the large, heavy bells hanging on stout leather straps rang out their joyous sounds. The cows, intent on filling their stomachs, ignored the music they were creating, but we were transported as surely as if we were outside a great cathedral listening to its bells calling people to worship.

A few moments later I returned from my reverie and heard once again the cry of the loons as they continued their conversation in the deepening twilight.

Reflection

Silence! The power is off, and all the little motors—the refrigerator, gas heater, heat exchanger in the fireplace—are still. No sound but the ticking of the clock and the fire crackling in the fireplace.

Even the wind has ceased rattling the windows. The trees stand dark and damp, their leaves hanging in sodden clumps. Fog sifts in shrouding the islands out of my existence. It is hard to tell where the river ends and the sky begins. They have taken on the same steely color.

I sit by the window in the half-light. Some might call it a gloomy day. I find it soft, luminous as a pearl—a time to cease all extraneous activity—to reflect. I need only a bit of heat from the fire to keep me warm, water saved in a pitcher before the power went off to quench my thirst, and a piece of fruit to relieve the pangs of hunger. I am forced into inactivity and it feels good—coming home to myself.

Life is suddenly reduced to food-clothing-shelter. How wonderful to be reminded of what little I actually need. For a while I am free to think about what is really important—healthy activity, love, relationships, the give and take of sharing.

If this power outage lasts long enough, perhaps I will be able to sort out the trivial from the meaningful activities, and bring my focus back to what is nurturing to my soul. Maybe I don't even need a power outage to do that.

The Olden Days

"Tell me about the olden days," begged twelve-year-old Melanie. I think I was in the midst of one of my "When I was your age" talks, and the expression, "olden days" stopped me mid-sentence. I suddenly felt ancient. Her "olden days" and mine were not the same.

When I thought about "olden days," I conjured up visions of ladies in bustles or hoop skirts carrying lace-trimmed parasols to protect them from the strong rays of the sun. Pictures of horse-drawn carriages, backyard water pumps, outhouses equipped with Sears-Roebuck catalogs, quilting parties, and barn-raisings came to my mind. I wondered what people did before the days of the telephone. How did they keep in close touch with their friends?

Melanie wondered what life was like before television. What did you do when you came home from school on a cold wintry day and there was no Mouseketeers program to watch, or Saturday morning cartoons before a leisurely breakfast?

Where did clean clothes come from if you didn't have an automatic washer and dryer? She couldn't imagine a car without a heater, automatic shift, or even a radio. Was there life before cars? How did you fix a cut if you didn't have a band-aid and some first-aid cream?

My, how times have changed! I wonder what visions will pop into the mind of her child when he says to her one day, "Tell me about the olden days."

Looking Or Finding

It was cold as I walked on the beach one morning on Sanibel. I met a man all bundled up in a heavy jacket, hat and gloves, his feet and legs encased in thick rubber boots. He held a long-handled net for scooping up sand and shells in the shallow water close to the shore. As I approached him, he blurted out, "It's mighty cold out here this morning—and there aren't any shells." He didn't look happy. I smiled, and agreed that it was a little chilly, and walked on, clutching my bag of shells.

I thought about that...There is a difference between looking for shells and finding shells. When I look for shells, I become so intent on the search, I forget to notice the rhythmic pattern of crashing waves, the variety of shore birds searching for their morning meal, or to feel the warm sun on my back. I don' t have time to say hello to other beach walkers. I might miss that special shell I have been searching for.

I have very decided ideas about what I should find in order to be successful. When I look, I become disappointed if I do not find. Though I may see many different kinds of shells, if they are not what I am looking for I ignore them, as if they didn't exist.

Even though I may arrive home with my bag full of shells, I'm never quite satisfied. There should always be more, if only I could have found that one elusive specimen!

Some days I just go to the beach to enjoy the sunrise, the freedom from mundane chores, the freshness of the ocean breeze, the chance to let my mind skitter, like the sandpipers, from one thought to another, unfettered by convention or preconceived notions.

With a grateful heart I thank the Divine Creator for the blessings of health, the joy of discovery and appreciation. I feel surrounded by the warmth of the Eternal Presence, and I begin to find shells. They just seem to appear at my feet. Since I have no predetermined expectations, I am pleased with anything I choose to pick up. I feel relaxed, open, and ready for any exchange with my fellow beachcombers. I take time to enjoy my surroundings.

When I arrive home I feel refreshed, enriched, and ready for whatever the rest of the day holds. My bag is filled with shells.

Seventy-Six And Who's Counting?

"Growing old is no more than a bad habit which a busy man has no time to form,"—Andre Maurois

"When you get to be my age, you'll know what I mean," bemoaned an unhappy client as she sat in my office one day several years ago. Of course I didn't tell her I was already five years older than she. In our conversations I often heard her say, "It's tough to get old—old age is creeping up on me," or, "I'm getting old—I can't do much any more."

All of these expressions are really self-fulfilling prophecies. Thinking she is getting old and less able predicts the premature outcome.

In an era when so much value and emphasis is placed on youth, I find it incredible that so many people complain openly about the pain of aging, bitterly resigning themselves to advancing debility. Others deny reality, and frantically buy into the latest method of youth retention.

But there are some people who were productively engaged in the act of living their lives to the fullest right up until the end and didn't seem to have time to think about getting old, and worrying about wrinkles and dumpy figures—Kathryn Hepburn and Mother Teresa. Even my sister-in-law at the age of eighty-nine still climbs into her little outboard motor boat on a calm day and drives around the St. Lawrence River. To her, osteoporosis just means that she is a few inches shorter than she used to be.

When I am actively pursuing a goal that has meaning for me—swimming, walking on the beach early in the morning, writing, reading, learning something new—I lose all sense of the passage of time. I forget about aches and pains, and I never tell myself that I am too old and cannot complete what I have started. I have boundless energy as long as I am focused, and only feel tired when I stop to think about what I have done, and decide that it was too much for one person to accomplish in a day.

I know it is important to take care of my body, the "temple of my soul." It would be unfortunate to have it fail me as a result of neglect or misuse before I have completed my life work. I also know that to spend hours trying to make it look as it did at age twenty-nine is a waste of time.

I conclude that old is a state of mind, not the sum total of years a person has been alive.

Beach-Find

What did I find on the beach at Sanibel today?

Space—to stretch my mind to its farthest reaches, and wonder what lies beyond. To feel the sun on my back, and know that it gives not only light and warmth, but life itself.

Time—to speak to Creation, and listen for a response. To walk as far as I want, and turn back only when I felt tired. To stand and look at a dead fish, and wonder where it was born, how old it was—was it sick long? Did it hurt to die? To stop and talk to two friendly newcomers to our island who wanted to know how far it was to Captiva, and could they walk there? To share their enthusiasm for sun and sand, sky and sea.

Freedom—to become nameless, and connect with pure being. To give up concern for what other people think about me—my hair blowing in the wind, shoes soaked by an unexpected wave, rumpled shorts with an unmatched T-shirt. To stay as long as I want—no one at home this day to worry about where I am.

Peace—that comes when I let go of those things I cannot change, and focus on the present moment. To celebrate life as it is—not as it was, or what I hope it will be.

I did find some empty shells—a turkey wing, moon shell, two left-handed whelks, some olive shells, so little and skinny I wondered how a creature could find room to live inside and move around.

I picked up a tiny horse conch, no longer alive, robbed by some unknown assailant of its chance to reach its full potential, like the children in Scotland who were cut down in their classroom by an unknown intruder before they had a chance to reach the prime of their lives.

I am full of all I found on the beach today.

River-Watch

I sit on the deck and watch the river. One by one, the waves wash against the shore. They don't hurry, but are always moving in a steady, relentless flow. As I watch, the waves don't tumble over each other, trying to get there first, but take their turn to reach the shore. They seem to have no ulterior motive—only a simple reaction to the force of the wind and what I imagine to be the pure joy of being in motion.

I doubt that the river plans its day. It just seems to respond to whatever comes—wind, rain, sunshine and clouds. It reflects the color of sky, and sparkles when the sun dances on its surface.

I don't think the river worries about what is in store for it tomorrow, nor does it weep and moan over what happened yesterday. All of its vast energies are focused on this present moment, and its actions are directly connected to whatever it has to face right now.

If I will listen to the voice of the river, perhaps I will cease worrying about what might happen tomorrow, or next week, or next year. I might even realize that what happened yesterday is now history and cannot be changed no matter how much time and energy I spend ruminating about what could have been.

I sit on the deck and watch the river. My soul is nourished, and I feel refreshed. However, if I ignore river's lessons, pollute it with my refuse, disregard its essential nature, we will both be diminished.

Surprise

I thought the winter of my life might become

    cold

    bleak

    full of losses

    narrowing down

    lonely

    fraught with unanswered questions

    realizing that I'm running out of time

    so frightening, I would want the relief of final escape.

Now I find the winter of my life is sprinkled with

    new and friendly faces

    time for gold and silver reflection

    loss of vanity, fear of failure, of being wrong, out of step, of worry about

        what others will think

    an awakening to new and unused talents

    a fresh awareness of all my blessings—good health, a loving family, kind

        and gentle companionship

time to discover a deeper appreciation of creation, an abiding relationship

    with Creator...

I am so busy living the winter of my life I have little time to feel

    cold

    bleak

    lonely

    frightened

The unanswered questions challenge me to keep stretching beyond the
visible horizon to dimensions felt only in the deeper regions of my
soul.

Where?

Where do thoughts come from? What causes me to select the words that make up these particular thoughts, which appear to be so uniquely, mine? I know I don't make them up by myself. When I pick up my pen to write, I often do not know what the finished product will be. What mysterious presence prompts me?

I look at a packet of seeds. The label says they are sweet peas, but these little bits of matter give no hint of what they will finally be. Only when they are planted in fertile soil and watered do they begin to unfold and become what they were destined to be.

Does the same mysterious energy which prompts the seed to become a sweet pea also direct the thoughts that form in my mind? I think so. Dare I call it God? Yes!

If I am correct, then with a force of such power and magnitude present, I have reason to be optimistic about the possibility for a world in which evil will finally be defeated, and love will emerge as the ruling spirit in the whole vast universe.

Win-Lose

Here in our cove the air is still, but far out on the river I can see ripples forming. The wind has shifted to the north and is beginning to blow. Our summer weather is coming to an end, and I feel sad.

Change is a part of life. There must be endings in order to have beginnings. If I had still, hot, sunny days continuously, I would become lethargic and bored with sameness. I notice a part of me is ready for what comes next.

Fall is on the way. Acorns are dropping from the oak trees. When they hit the top of my car, they sound like a shot from a gun.

But where are the squirrels—gray, black? At this time of year they are usually scampering around in great numbers, gathering their nuts for the winter.

I have been told that there are now more eagles around the islands, and they may have devoured most of the squirrels. That, too, has brought about change. I love to watch eagles soaring, but I miss the squirrels. Why can't I have it both ways—eagles and squirrels?

Have we humans so over-populated and over-developed the world that nature can no longer bring things into proper balance? Will we humans, who have always tried to win out over nature, finally be the ultimate losers?

Sunset

Without a sound, the river gently caresses the shore, gliding by on its way to the sea. Even the gulls have ceased their screaming. They float on the water or fly silently by.

This is a rare occurrence on my busy river—not a single boat has come by in the last quarter-hour to break the silence.

I'm afraid to breathe for fear of disturbing this gentle scene.

A few moments ago the sun cast a brilliant path of white light across the water, ending on the shore in front of me. Now, as it sinks slowly behind the islands, the horizon takes on a golden glow, turning to vibrant orange, and then fiery red. I see purple, mauve, lavender, and a touch of green. The clouds are outlined in bright pink. All this color spreads quickly across the sky as far as I can see. What a magnificent palette of colors!

Once the sun has set, the after-glow is even more brilliant than ever. Tonight, it will be at least two hours before the last bit of color fades into the black of night. I breathe a prayer of thanksgiving for such a gift.

Now I retreat to the warmth of my house, for the air has become crisp. I am reminded that though it is still early in September, summer has ended here on Wellesley Island. Frosty nights will soon follow.

I live with the promise of many memorable sunsets to come. Will any surpass the one I have just witnessed?

Soon, I will travel south to escape the cold winds and the ice and snow. But before I leave I walk the now-deserted roads in the state park, basking in the autumn sun, tasting the crisp, clear air of fall. My eyes drink in once again the glorious array of colored leaves. As I walk along, I see a few squirrels and chipmunks scampering about gathering nuts and seeds for winter feasting. Deer are fattening up in the meadows as they prepare for the lean months ahead.

I feel a subtle sense of urgency about all activities in the shortening days, but I also experience a quiet slowing down. There are fewer boats on the river. Visitors and cottagers have left, and there is more time for aloneness and meditation. For me, this is a necessary refueling time.

1999

While here I stand, not only with the sense
Of present pleasure, but with pleasing thoughts
That in this moment there is life and food
For future years.

<u>Lines</u>—composed a few miles above
Tintern Abby—July 13, 1798
William Wordsworth

Morning Walk

The days of late April grow hot and humid here on Sanibel. I begin to long for the fresh, crisp air of early spring, and the sound of the river lapping against the shore in front of our summer cottage on Wellesley Island. Soon we will leave Florida for another season on the St. Lawrence River.

Meanwhile, this morning I walked on the bike path along Periwinkle Way, feeling alone and at odds with my spirit. It was warm and I was hurrying to get to the bookstore. A young woman on a bicycle approached from the opposite direction—quite ordinary looking, eyes downcast, intent on her riding. She looked up at me and smiled as she passed. Her face lit up like a sunflower raising its head to the light—transformed from ordinary to extraordinary. I smiled in return. That felt good.

A few minutes later I encountered another lady—much older; her face a map of wrinkles, thinning white hair frizzled around her head like a halo. Skinny legs with knobby knees pedaled rhythmically along the way. Gnarled hands grasped the handlebars intent on steering a straight course. When she saw me she beamed rays of sunshine that permeated my whole being.

After a few minutes I began to notice something warm and fuzzy happening to me. My body relaxed. I lengthened my stride, lifted my chin, and looked at the canopy of trees hovering over my head. I saw a variety of shapes and shades of green, flowers I hadn't noticed before. The sounds of traffic faded, and I heard bird songs.

God spoke to me this morning!

The Lesson

My days are hurried, harried, full to the limit. I feel tense, anxious and overwhelmed. I wonder why.

Outside my window the lake is a mirror. Trees stand still and silent. Clouds hang in the sky, unmoving.

It suddenly occurs to me that lake, trees, clouds are doing nothing more than existing in the present. They have left behind the wind of yesterday. Tomorrow's challenge does not exist. There is only this one, quiet moment.

Is this a clue for me? Am I hanging onto my "wind of yesterday?" Do I spend my energy cramming all my commitments for the next two weeks into this one present moment? No wonder I feel harried and overwhelmed!

Do I have the sense to quiet this scrambling mind in order to use this powerful lesson?

Nature teaches me valuable lessons if only I will listen to her. But she does not insist. It is up to me to watch, listen and to learn from her example.

Speak Up!

"Speak up." They said. "Your voice is too low/" I couldn't believe they were talking to me. My mental image of myself doesn't fit with what they were saying. Memories of the loud-mouthed, ungainly kid who felt stupid in the classroom, climbed trees and played football with the boys are still so strong I have trouble thinking of myself as a quiet-speaking adult.

I remember well the little kids in the neighborhood who came to me for protection against the bully on the block when he threatened them. He never had to ask me to speak up. He also learned to give me a wide berth during after-school playtime.

All humans, in the first years of their lives, construct a mental picture of themselves, based on their reactions to early experiences and the response of others significant to them. Many will periodically review that image and update it to fit their more current conditions and feelings about themselves. But others will continue to hold onto that first picture as if it were set in concrete and unchangeable.

It took me many years to discover that what I thought about myself did not fit with my more current situation, and how others view me. I slowly woke up to the fact that I am not a loudmouth dummy. I have an open, inquiring mind, and I actually possess a body of knowledge worthy of sharing with anyone interested in listening.

So, speak up. Your voice is too low!

Salvation?

Like the bees that buzz from blossom to blossom gathering nectar, my mind flits from one image to another, recalling past impressions, feelings, experiences, memories. Unlike the honeybee, I don't know what the end result will be.

How do I make sense of the ugliness of war as I watch the glow of a sunrise in a multi-colored sky?

What do I do with hate that drives students to gun down their classmates when I know that most desperately angry people leave an obvious trail of clues before they act out their fury?

How do I reconcile the multi-million dollar contract signed by an athlete not yet graduated from college, with the salary of a teacher struggling to provide for his family a decent standard of living?

What about peace, justice, mercy and equality? Are they just fantasies conjured up by a dreamer of the impossible, never to be realized in my lifetime or the next?

I listen to my daughter explain to her angry eight-year-old son the mood swings of his teacher in her third trimester of pregnancy. "One minute she yells at us," he blurts out, "and the next minute she is all lovey-dovey!" Because he is able to talk about his feelings with a sympathetic adult, he becomes more willing to see the other side of the story. Andrew is learning to be understanding and tolerant, and to forgive his teacher her occasional inconsistencies.

I know it is possible to teach little children how to deal with their anger and get along with people who are different and sometimes disagreeable. I also know that if left to their own devices, they will accept quite naturally a wide range of differences in other people.

The key to the salvation of our species and our world may very well be in the hands of the children who are capable of creating what seems so elusive to me—peace and good will among all people.

Midnight Splendor

Last night something woke me in the middle of the night. The moon shone through my window, so bright I could see the hands on the clock next to my bed. I rose to see a path of silvery white light shimmering across the mirrored river. The ancient oaks in the front yard stood silently in the still night air. I heard geese honking somewhere in the distance. All was calm and peaceful.

In the midst of all this splendor, it was hard for me to realize that halfway around the world bombs were falling on a troubled land. The same moon that dazzled me must have been shining over there.

I wonder—what is the matter with us humans, that we can be so blind to the beauty that surrounds us, and to the sacredness of all life? There must be a better way to settle differences than to tear up the countryside, pollute the land and endanger the lives of millions of people.

After awhile I returned to my bed with hope in my heart that one day, through each of us, the plan of Creation will ultimately be realized, and we will learn to live in harmony with each other, with the moon that shines on all the earth, the trees, the still and running waters, the geese and all the other creatures in the world.

Red Bird

Outside my window this morning a red bird sings to me:

Good morning

A lovely day

How great to be alive!

With his mate nearby, he sings with pure bliss. I feel transported from earthly

concerns to a sense of joy, calm and peace.

My spirit soars far from thinking, planning and determining, into the realm of

quiet observation:

A tiny striped butterfly flitting across the grass

The intricate beauty of a pink blossom

Maple leaves open to balmy sunlight

Pine needles gracefully dancing in a gentle breeze

The splash of a fish jumping in the river.

I am blessed with the wonder of it!

Battle

This morning I got into a fight with my hair. I wanted it to settle into a particular pattern.

My hair said, "Nah, I don't want to do that."

I pulled my hairbrush through the errant strands, wielded the hair dryer with determination, and said, "You will move in this direction."

My hair said. "NO!"

After ten minutes of pulling and tugging, I had to admit defeat. My hair won that battle.

Finally, I said, "OK, hair where do you want to go?"

My hair said, "This way. I need to follow my instincts. I just want you to understand that I have feelings, and a real sense of what is right for me. Pay attention and I will lead you."

And do you know? My hair was right. As soon as I gave up the fight, and paid attention, everything went well. I even liked the results.

Loss

The oak tree in my front yard is slowly dying. It was badly damaged by the ice storm in January, 1998. Several of its limbs were broken by the weight of the ice. Others were left dangling dangerously and had to be removed. For many years that tree provided shade from the late afternoon sun. Now there are gaping holes where the sun pours in on us as we dine in the early evening light.

The wish to return to an earlier time when life seemed simpler and more ideal is strong. Memory often distorts reality, and we think it was better then. I know I had more shade "back when," but I also could see less of the river. Now, when a lovely big sailboat goes by, I can track its passage uninhibited by low-hanging branches.

Finally, after a period of bemoaning my loss of shade, I bought a sunscreen curtain to pull down over the big window late in the afternoon when the sun is low in the sky. I can still see the river, but the rays of the sun are filtered. Dinnertime is once again a comfortable and pleasurable experience.

I may lose my oak tree some time in the near future. I will miss its towering presence.

Nature reminds me once again that change is an integral part of life. Nothing ever remains the same. When I finally accept this facet of reality, I become free to adjust creatively to the new circumstances in my life.

Trivia

Sun sparkles on the water like hundreds of clear crystal beads. The river in its relentless flow to the sea seems not to notice what happens on its surface. It allows the sun to play on it, but will not be delayed. It journeys on.

Some days the rain pelts down and the wind whips the water into powerful waves that may cause the river to appear as though it has changed direction. It refuses to be distracted. It continues to move inexorably northward.

No external events or transient conditions raise any question about its final destination.

There is a lesson in this for me.

I sometimes let the trivia of everyday living seep into the core of my being and confuse me about the authenticity of my soul's journey. I begin to wonder where I am going, and raise the question: "Is it all right for me to follow my destiny, regardless of what happens on the surface of my life? And, what is my destiny anyway?"

These ruminations sap my energy and steal hours from my days. I don't like that. I am giving up valuable time that I can never get back.

Like the river with its singular intent, perhaps I can grant the surface events of my life only their just due, and allow Creator to direct me back to the path I am intended to travel.

That's Wrong

I stood on the beach and watched an ibis poking her long orange beak into the sand at the edge of the water. "Her knees are on backward," I said to myself. "That's wrong." Farther down the beach I saw a snowy egret walking along, suffering from the same affliction.

I thought about all the other things in the world that are wrong. I'm left-handed. I learned a long time ago that this is wrong, so I switched to writing with my right hand. But I couldn't change everything. I iron left-handed. Now my iron is wrong. The cord comes out the side next to me and gets in my way.

The people in England drive on the wrong side of the road. I almost got killed once when I stepped off the curb into traffic coming down the wrong side of the street.

My best friend in sixth grade grew up on the wrong side of the tracks. She was nice, but her address wasn't.

Republicans—Democrats—Independents. Who is right?

The list goes on and on. How can I live comfortably with so much wrong in the world?

Then I look back at the ibis. She pokes along filling her stomach with all the good food she finds in the sand. Her legs still don't function like mine, but she doesn't notice. They work just fine for her.

I wonder. Do I really know enough to determine what is right for some one else? Perhaps my ability to live in peaceful co-existence will depend more on my willingness to accept the differences in this world, than on trying to figure out who is right and who is wrong.

Now

Each day that dawns is a new beginning, but only if I can let go of yesterday. Why can't I learn from the birds I see scurrying along the beach or flapping through the trees, hunting for today's meal? They don't sit on a branch worrying about how hungry they were yesterday, or about what happened to the neighborhood loud-mouth who sang his heart out every morning in the tree next door. What might happen tomorrow or two weeks from now is of no concern to them. They live with all their energies focused on the now.

Life is a never-ending process, and I cannot stop the natural progression of this process by denying its existence—or feeling guilty about yesterday—or worrying about tomorrow. If I tried, I would only miss the opportunity to deal creatively with this particular phase of my life.

Nowhere can this continual process be seen more clearly than in Nature. Nothing is ever lost, only changed. And all that happens takes place in the present moment. A tulip starts life as a bulb; it grows into a plant, produces a bud, which develops into a beautiful flower. That flower is not permanent; it soon withers and dies. The foliage continues to produce energy, which is sent back to the bulb to be used to produce next year's flower. So, the cycle continues.

We watch winter come to an end. The whole world appears momentarily suspended in time. The woods stand silently, patiently waiting for new life to emerge. The outward appearance is one of death, but deep within, the juices of life are stirring and beginning to flow. They are sluggish at first, then gradually pick up speed until there is a final surge, and spring bursts forth. Re-birth! Another new beginning. It has been happening as long as the earth has been in existence. And it all happens in the present moment.

To live my life in the now—to be open to the spirit, and the nature of things, is to be in the presence of a power of great beneficence.

Thoughts In The Early Morning

We human beings are so resistant to learning. We are impatient, unknowing, unwilling, stubborn. Mostly, we are afraid. We don't realize we will never be given more than we can handle. So, some of us, in our abject fear, resort to drugs to create a false sense of beauty, peace, tranquility, or expansiveness and excitement. Some turn to alcohol to escape what we fear the most. Others become psychotic and retreat to a fantasy world where we no longer have to deal with anything. A few commit suicide, which to them, appears to be the final escape.

Most of us just build walls to protect ourselves—to make us feel safe. We become rich and surround ourselves with things in order to feel secure. But always there is the fear that we will lose what we own; someone will take it, or it won't be enough. We continue to chase after more.

Some of us collect people—relationships to help us feel secure—someone who will be obliged to take care of us, who will worship or respect us so we can feel good; someone always to be with us so we won't have to face ourselves and our own mortality.

Others of us create or buy into an elaborate and rigid set of rules by which to live our lives, and with which we can force others to live their lives—so we can feel secure. Life then would be constant and predictable. Presumably there would be no surprises. We have to believe there is only one way to think, and our way is right. To be wrong or just different would be to lose a sense of self, and that would be intolerable.

Some of us are so lacking in love and respect for ourselves and others, we spend a lifetime doing hateful things, crushing all that is good and decent along the way.

However, if we look closely, there are always a few of us who seem to have caught a vision of that grand scheme created by the Master Himself, and are living our lives according to His will for us—in peace and love, and in service to others.

Live, Death Will Wait

Death walked in one day
Smiled, and took me by the hand
I pulled away and said,
"No, not yet! I have many things to do before I walk with you:
words to write
relationships to nurture
challenges to face
questions to ask
answers to seek.
"Creation, do I have enough time to do all this?"

"You have eternity, and yet, not a moment to waste—
live exuberantly
create with vision
experience fervently
relate with feeling
Rise with the sun—sleep under a blanket of stars—dream beyond limits."

"Death will come again when the time is right."

Death

The sunset spreads orange and gold across the horizon. A sliver of moon hovers off my left shoulder and leaves a path of white light across the water. Stars appear in the deepening darkness.

My breathing quiets as my spirit attempts to match the serenity of the moment. I watch in humble awareness.

The trees stand silent and peaceful; their leaves hang with the stillness of death, waiting for the fall. But before they finish their full season, they will be arrayed in a riot of color—a final celebration of life, and a sure promise of resurrection.

For many years, with a slight sense of foreboding, I watched this happen. Now, I no longer mourn the loss, but marvel at the glory of transformation from life to death, and to life again.

I cannot doubt the loving nature of the Divine Creator. Nothing, or no one could create such beauty in anger, jealousy, disillusionment or vengeance. I, and all humankind must be very special to have been given the sense to experience and appreciate the awesome nature of the universe.

I bow my head in thanksgiving.

2000

"What mighty battles have I seen and heard
waged between the trees and the west wind—
an Iliad fought in the fields of air."

Edith M. Thomas

Tribute

✦

Elizabeth Pyke Stamp

1908–2000

The joy of returning to my beloved St. Lawrence river after a winter of balmy weather, sea breezes and sandy beaches on Sanibel is somewhat subdued this year. Our matriarch of Grand View, Elizabeth Pyke Stamp, is no longer with us.

Charles' sister had been a member of our small community for most of her life. At ninety-one years of age, that's a long time. She loved to regale us with fascinating stories of Grand View when it was a primitive little group of cottages. The only access to the island was by boat or a two-car ferry that chugged across a narrow strip of the river from sun-up to sundown. If you missed the last ferry, you stayed on the mainland until the next day.

In those days, with no electricity, Aladdin lamps provided light for the evening hours, and the town pump was the source of water for drinking, cooking and washing dishes. It was also a gathering place to catch up on the latest community news.

One of my favorite memories is watching Elizabeth start out for her morning walk to the state park with her little dog in tow, getting her daily exercise. Wherever she went around Grand View, Julie followed, tugging at the end of a firmly held leash.

At an age when many grandmothers take to their rocking chairs, Elizabeth could still be found checking on the condition of her dock, and, when necessary, pounding nails into a loose board. It never occurred to her that old ladies didn't usually do that kind of work. She loved the water, and swam daily back and forth between the docks.

Elizabeth owned a small motor boat. On a calm day, she often drove around the river by herself, just to enjoy the beauty of her beloved islands.

A few years ago, urged on by friends and family, Elizabeth published a book, Glimpses of Grand View, which included a history of the community and a collection of stories by some of the local residents. Her background in journalism served her well, and we now have a wonderful record, in words and pictures, of our small but cherished section of the magnificent Thousand Islands.

Elizabeth left us a valuable legacy of love and respect for our river home. We all will miss her.

Change

This morning, as I walk through the quiet and empty state park, I find myself surrounded by the soft new green of late spring. It looks as fresh as a crisp, green salad. It is a special green, found at no other time of the year. The trees bask in their lovely new clothes, grasses and wild flowers are thriving, and the ferns are unfolding new fronds. All is pristine, untouched by wind and storm.

Though the air is nippy, the sky is a clear, deep blue, and the river sparkles in the early sunshine.

I look at the mounds of Precambrian rocks on the side of the road, and speculate about their age—older than the melting glacier that formed this exquisite area. As I walk along, I realize that I am in the midst of one of the geological wonders of the world, the amazing Thousand Islands.

Having read some of the history of these islands, I realize that underlying all the other things that happened here, this whole area developed for one grand reason—to give people the opportunity to get away from the fast pace of city life—a chance to "smell the roses", pick a few daisies, and to meditate and relate directly to the awesome wonders of nature.

All of this is about to change unless there is a united and concerted effort to forestall the latest scheme to destroy forever the quiet beauty and ambience of this area. I refer, of course, to the proposal to build a huge gambling casino and resort complex at the east end of Wellesley Island, with all the attendant noise, traffic jams, neon glitz and litter that accompanies massive concentrations of human beings.

I cannot imagine that anyone who takes the time to research the devastation wreaked by the presence of a gambling casino in places like

Atlantic City, Oneida, Lake Tahoe, to name a few with which I am familiar, could believe that such a facility would be an asset to the area. Yes, you can go to the above cities and see the lovely condominiums, fancy mansions, "gorgeous" casinos with their fine restaurants and other amenities, but if you happen to approach the area by the back road, you will see boarded-up once-thriving businesses and restaurants, abandoned houses where the former owners could no longer afford to make their mortgage payments, and all the other signs of poverty.

I wonder who will patronize Bonnie Castle, the Riveredge, Cavallarios, and all the other fine local restaurants, when for considerably less money they will be able to go to the casino and fill their stomachs at the same time that they empty their pockets of the week's grocery money and the monthly mortgage payments.

I pray for a sane and responsible solution to the current issue so close to the hearts of so many of us whose families have lived among the Thousand Islands for generations, and others who have more recently discovered the magic of this special place.

Gems

Each new day is a precious gem that comes to me as a gift; and every one is different. One is bright, crystal clear, a lovely delicate azure. One may be dark, cloudy and rough. Another is soft, misty, and pearly gray. Still another is changeable, depending on how I look at it. Part will be clear and shining, part swirling with darkness and angry clouds.

If I am to enjoy them, I must appreciate all of them for their variety and uniqueness. I realize each one has a purpose, and it is for me to discover and accept what that purpose is.

Something I am learning about gems is that their beauty is enhanced when they are appropriately used. I will do different things with different gems. I would never go swimming with a pearl around my neck, nor would I go on a picnic on a dark, cloudy rough day. But a pearl on a simple black dress when I go to a party would be exquisite. And I might wander off to the beach in my boots and rain gear to marvel at the power and grandeur of Mother Nature in a particularly angry mood; or perhaps, sit quietly by the fire with a good book, and enjoy the solitude.

Again, I discover the value and beauty of a gem is magnified when it is shared. If I hide it in a box, it will only languish with potential beauty and value. If I share it with others, it will come into its full glory, and be a joy to everyone who beholds it.

I have many gems in my memory box, and each one has taught me a valuable lesson, though I haven't always known it. The bright, clear azure ones are easy; they are simply there to be enjoyed, appreciated, marveled at. It is the dark, cloudy, rough ones that require a great deal of hard work, and from which I can learn much. I must first be aware of their value; then I must polish and scrub, and file away the rough spots until they, too, begin to glow with their beauty.

Ah, how wonderful are gems! I don't know how many I have left, but I will relish each one as if it were the only one.

Impermanence

While I walked in the woods one morning, observing the world around me, an interesting thought came into my mind—life is like a fatal disease. Once you have it, the ultimate outcome is always the same—you're going to die. In the case of cancer, heart disease, Alzheimer's disease, Parkinson's disease, and more recently AIDS, to name just a few, humans have spent vast sums of money, and countless man-hours, trying to discover a cure for these afflictions so they will not have to die—at least from these causes.

It seems to me that many people treat life in much the same way. A great deal of time and money is spent on various schemes in a futile and frantic attempt to deny, or at least forestall, the inevitable outcome; from Ponce de Leon in his search for the Fountain of Youth, all the way to cosmetic counters around the world where sales people hawk their wares and their promises of eternal youth, if not in actuality, at least in surface appearance.

Such a waste of time, effort, money! If we humans could ever get to the point of truly accepting our own mortality, as a natural part of the life experience, we would finally be free to give our selves fully to the process of living and growing.

I do not mean to discredit the importance of medical research designed to relieve the suffering of individuals so they may live their lives fruitfully, with reasonable longevity, and as comfortably as possible. In fact, I applaud the efforts to increase the life expectancy of humans, and to enhance the physical quality of life.

But when I come face to face with the concept of impermanence, and embrace it as one of the eternal truths of the universe, I will let go of my grasping, and hanging on, my fear of the unknown, the different, and rejoice in the fullness of each day. I will reach out and savor all the possibilities for experiences and relationships this moment holds for me. I can let go of the past and move confidently into the future. I know what the ultimate outcome is. If I think about it at all, I will wonder what the possibilities are for me in that final experience.

New Growth

On a hill in the state park there stands a tall, once-stately old pine tree. Its lower branches are broken off, with stumps of varying lengths protruding from the straight trunk. Midway up the trunk a few scraggly still-alive limbs sway lethargically—but at the very top of the tree, life is vigorous and abundant. Short green branches crowd together, covered with dark green needles. The tips of these new branches display long spikes of new growth. From where I stand, they appear to be eight to ten inches long.

I'm intrigued by the evidence of the will to live in such an aged specimen, and revel in the significance of this powerful lesson for me. It really is never too late for new growth.

I think about older clients who came to me for counseling some years back. Some of them seemed so defeated, buffeted about by the winds of time and circumstance. It did not occur to them that there was still room in their lives for accommodation and growth. In many cases, their reason for coming to me was to get me to bring about some kind of change in their environment so they could at least be more comfortable, if not happy. The possibility that they could change the way they looked at their lives, that they might still be able to grow in new and different directions was not part of their thinking.

But there were some people who clung tenaciously to the will to live, and like the pine tree, developed new branches that led to growth, keeping them actively involved in their world.

As I look at the top of that ancient tree, I wonder what the possibilities for new growth for me will be when I can no longer walk in the woods, ride my bike, work in my garden and swim in the water. Will I find a way to ignore my "broken branches" and move on to new ways to exercise that part of me that can still grow? I'm working on that right now.

Patriotism

Patriotism—what does it mean to be patriotic? Do I say, "My country, right or wrong?" Or do I demand that it be all it can possibly be, even if that means taking an unpopular stand, sometimes disagreeing with national policy?

Would I defend my child in all instances, no matter what crime he committed, or would I insist that he be responsible for his actions, and accept the consequences of his choices?

What about myself? Do I stumble blindly on, destroying my own life, and all else that gets in my way, and then whine and cry over the results, insisting it is not my fault? Would I demand that everyone respect me, regardless of my activities, or whether I had earned that respect?

How do I demonstrate my love and loyalty to myself, my child, my country?

True love requires that I accept others and myself right where we are now, knowing that at any given moment we all do the best we can. But I also think that love gives me the insight to recognize the potential for growth and prosperity through peaceful co-existence inherent in each of us, and urges me to encourage and expect that this potential will be a part of all striving. I cannot sit quietly by when my child, my country, or I fail to recognize this.

A mother lion instinctively assumes the responsibility for the protection and nurturing of her cubs. She proceeds with a caring attitude toward herself and an unquestioning confidence in her own ability. The lessons she teaches are vital to the survival of her species. She expects her cubs to learn and will brook no laziness or inattention. With much loving encouragement and an occasional cuff of reprimand, those cubs do learn, and ultimately assume full responsibility for themselves in the world of nature.

Surely, I can learn from that lioness and accept the fact that my worth was already established at the moment of my birth. Though I may not have learned the lessons of self-love and respect as a child, I have the potential for learning them now.

If I truly love my child, I will teach her to love and respect herself. On her road to becoming she will learn to be considerate, cooperative, and competent. My method must be benevolent, firm and insistent. The very survival of our human species may depend on the world's children learning the lesson of living peacefully with all other creatures.

I begin to see that patriotism is an expression of love. If I love my country, I will not follow blindly the dictates of unloving, narrow-minded, and self-seeking leaders. I will insist that its greatness depends not on unfair advantage or military strength, but rather, is in direct proportion to its willingness to work for a world of mutual respect, a world of peaceful co-existence, and one in which all nations can strive to reach their own destiny. World survival may very well depend on our success.

After The Rain

After the rain—the woods are washed clean. The wind blows lightly, rustling the still-wet leaves on the trees. Bright green moss glistens on damp rocks. Tree trunks, black with moisture, stand in sharp contrast with the lush green all around.

Gray clouds scud across the sky speckled with a few bright patches of blue. My father used to say that if there was enough blue to make a Dutchman a pair of breeches, it would be a nice day. He never did tell me how big the Dutchman might be.

So far, this has been a cool, wet, windy summer. The river is too cold for lengthy lap swimming. Ah, me! How awful!

Then I begin to think about what I have to celebrate. The grass in my yard was never more thick and green, and my flowers were never more beautiful. The ferns across the back of my house and in the woods are knee-high and luxurious. Wild flowers bloom everywhere in great abundance. I may not be able to swim as much as I would like, but I can walk in the State Park, even on a cool windy day.

I can sit and grump about what is "wrong" with this summer, or I can cultivate a heightened awareness of the goodness and bounty of "Mother Earth." I can bemoan the emptiness of my half-full glass, or enjoy the nectar in the part that is full. Which will I choose?

Paradox

A paradox—I am at once created and creator. The Eternal Creator is in me and I in Her. To worship a "God out there," apart from me is, I believe, the ultimate misunderstanding, and carries with global implications.

Unless I can truly comprehend that I am an integral part of the whole, vast universe, I cannot fully commit myself to helping solve the problems of global warming, oil spills in Alaska, starving children in the world, and poverty in third world countries, Appalachia, and the inner cities of my own country.

As a matter of fact, when I use the term, "my own country," I am already separating myself from the rest of the world. I see a need for a new vocabulary to even begin talking about universal concerns.

Before I would spray my house to kill spiders that spin webs around my windows, I had better learn something about the delicate balance of nature, and the natural food chain so important to that balance. I can't even step on a caterpillar without thinking that some bird might like it for breakfast.

We are all involved. I must connect with you, and you with me, if we will save our world and ourselves. The solution to a local problem, no matter how small, must include a consideration of the consequences to the whole, if we are to live in community with our Universal Mother—Earth!

To Love Myself?

What does it mean—to love myself? All through my growing years I received messages telling me how to think about myself. "Let others go first. Don't take the last piece. Children should be seen and not heard. You don't need that." And many more.

How could I care about myself when I was constantly being told that it was "more blessed to give than to receive?" In fact, it wasn't "blessed" to receive at all; it was downright selfish.

When I got older, I went to communion at church. There I learned that I was "not worthy so much as to gather up the crumbs under the Lord's table." I never wanted the crumbs under anyone's table! But here I was, being told I was too unworthy anyway. I had some pretty bad thoughts about the Lord until I realized that it was people saying those things—not the Lord.

Since I have become aware of my connectedness to the Eternal Spirit—the Creator of all that is—the expression, "God is Love" has come alive for me. If I have been created by, and am a part of that Spirit, then I must also be a part of that Love. There is a purpose and meaning in everything Spirit has created, and no such thing as unworthy. Now I can look into the mirror and be glad. It is my job to take care of me, to nurture this life I have been given. I will listen and respond to my own needs, even when others disagree. I will follow my own path, though I am pushed in a different direction by a thousand discordant voices. As long as I remain faithful to Creation, I cannot go wrong.

I am not unmindful of the needs of others. Part of the nurturing on my own spirit will include a loving concern for the interdependence of all living beings. But I believe Eric Fromm when he says in The Art Of Loving, that it is impossible to love another until I first love me.

Some time ago I watched a mother hawk feed her young. She took a piece of meat from a neighbor's outstretched hand, flew to the top of a utility pole and carefully examined it, apparently making sure it was all right. After eating what she wanted, she took the remains to her nest and fed her babies. That seemed a selfish thing to do—filling her own stomach while her hungry babies waited. Or was it? She knew, without caring what I thought, that she could best serve them by first serving her own needs. You might say, she loved herself enough to listen to the rhythm of her own body.

Nature surrounds me with powerful lessons!

The Nature of Things

One summer day, six-year-old Kendra came in from playing in the woods, covered with red welts, and said,

"Grandma, I know God made everything, but what good are mosquitoes?"

After some contemplation, I replied,

"I know they bite, and are a nuisance to humans, Kendra, but they are food for frogs, turtles and birds."

In the years since that little exchange, I have often pondered the nature of the universe, how it is, and how it came to be. As I look at the world around me, I realize that Creator has made nothing bad or useless. We humans often fail to see the intrinsic value in all things, but if we are willing to look with a wider perspective, we will see order and meaning, and yes, beauty in all that we have been given.

A shell that I picked up on the beach at Sanibel one morning last winter was covered with barnacles. I nearly passed it by. Stooping to examine it more closely, I discovered it was intact. If I would be willing to scrape away those barnacles, I could uncover its intrinsic beauty.

Similarly, a little child may appear ugly, covered with anger, resentment and bad manners. My tendency is to pass him by, to judge him to be unworthy of my attention. But if I look more closely at this child, disregard the surface behavior, and respond to his need for love, attention and acceptance, I might uncover the beauty that lies within.

Gems of Experience

As the sun rises above the horizon bringing assurance of respite from the blackness of night, so do I receive from the light of the Divine Presence the promise of deliverance from the darkness that sometimes surrounds my spirit.

I look at this new day with wonder and awe. The possibilities are without limit, the opportunities almost endless. It all depends on the choices I make.

I can limit my sights, strive for that rare, exotic mountaintop experience, believing such experiences are all there is in life of any value. With such limited vision, I will miss the daisies along the path, tiny new sprouts of spring carrying with them promises of new life.

I will not hear the laughter of children at play, the gurgling of a little brook wending its way down the mountain-side, the cry of a blue jay winging through the trees. Nor will I notice the glorious riot of color splashing across hillsides in October. I will miss the first blanket of snow covering the gray of November.

No, I tell myself, I am looking for something real, exciting, awe-inspiring, and worthy of God's attention, something I can carry with me for the rest of my life.

I forget that the air on the top of the mountain, as beautiful as the view might be, is so thin and chilly that hardly anything grows there. If I look carefully, I will see growing in the valley that which really sustains life. It is where we harvest food to nourish our bodies; where water from mountain streams collects to refresh the parched land; where people live who provide opportunities for relationships, for love, service.

This day is made of hundreds of tiny gems of experience that create a continuing source of replenishment for a hungry soul. Just as the body cannot exist on one stupendous banquet that may occur only rarely, neither can the spirit remain healthy and growing by relying on peak experiences that may happen only two or three times in a lifetime.

I have much to learn as this day unfolds. I pray that I will not miss a single opportunity.

Weather

Rain falls relentlessly on the already drenched land. Flowers droop under their heavy load of water. A white curtain of mist hangs over the river shrouding the islands in a dark gray cloak of anonymity. A lone heron flies in to land gracefully on the soggy dock—so intent on fishing for his breakfast that he seems not to notice the pounding rain. His coat must be waterproof, for moments later he takes off across the river unencumbered by the weight of soaked feathers.

No boat breaks the smooth, murky surface of the river this morning—a good day for sleeping in. All is still. The silence is palpable.

As I sit here in the gloom, listening for the sound of thunder, I try to decide whether it's safe to go swimming. Rain is no deterrent. Lightning sends me scurrying for cover.

Weather is a great equalizer. It causes us all to adjust our daily schedules according to its dictates. No one has an unfair advantage.

Is this a lesson for us? Can we possibly, some day, agree that all living beings are equally adored by Creator, and begin to act as though it were so?

I believe our survival as a human species depends on our learning how to celebrate and encourage that spark of divinity in every human being, starting with little children.

Elections

In the past few weeks the political conventions have occupied many hours of television time. I have listened to glorious rhetoric, elegant promises and a magnificent word picture of the Utopian world our country will be, if only I will vote for the right candidate.

I'm not sure that this is a particularly American ritual, but our brand of democracy lends itself to the current scene every four years. Millions of dollars are spent promoting the virtues of each candidate. When all is said, I don't find myself any more enlightened about the true nature of any of them. But I do know that each one wants the position, for whatever private or public reason, so badly that he or she is willing to risk a great deal to get there.

I'm saddened to realize that I am faced with voting against a particular candidate rather than for someone whom I think has the wisdom, intellectual capacity and integrity to bring our country into significant and honorable world leadership.

However, I cherish the opportunity to live in a country where I am relatively free to live my life according to my values, and with minimal interference.

Whatever the shortcomings of our present election process, I am profoundly grateful for the right, the privilege and the responsibility to cast my private vote for whomever I choose.

I will go to the polls in November.

The Lesson of the Trees

When I get up in the morning, I look out my window and see trees—stately, towering trees—so tall I would have to go outside to see the tops. From every window in my house I look out upon trees, flowers and grass.

I realize that every day of my life I see these marvels of nature and often take them for granted.

Living with the forest at my back and the river in front, I am reminded of how closely we humans are connected to all of life. When any part of that life is diminished, I too am diminished.

When I pollute with my waste the water in the river, I can no longer use it for drinking. When I clear-cut the trees in the mountains, I cannot stop the erosion of valuable top soil. If I obliterate a single species of animal, bird or fish, I interfere with the efficiency of the food chain.

When I devalue another human being with indifference, prejudice and intolerance, I stunt my own growth and limit my capacity for compassion and acceptance.

My goodness! I did not know I could learn so much from a tree. How deprived are the thousands of children who grow up in the concrete jungles of inner cities, and spend their lives never having lived with, and learned the lesson of the trees!

2001

Sail round the corner there may wait,
A new road, or a secret gate.

J.R.R. Tolkien

Half Full or Half Empty?

It occurs to me that to always look at a half-full glass and see only the empty part, is to live constantly with a feeling of deprivation.

As I get older, there are things I cannot do that I did with ease a few years ago. I can no longer run. My back hurts—but who needs to run? I am now retired and have time to plan ahead, so I can choose a leisurely pace to go wherever I want.

I cannot keep up with the rest of the Sanibel bike club when we go on rides together. No matter—most of the time I ride by myself, slowly, so I can meditate along the path, enjoy the scenery and "smell the roses." I'm thankful every day that I am still able to ride.

My hearing is not as sharp as it was ten years ago. It's nice to be able to smile and let some of the cocktail-hour drivel go right over my head. I think I don't miss anything important, and my friends always manage to communicate with me.

The "Golden Years" are not something I can look forward to. They're already here. But I now have a keener sense of the value of my present moment than I did years ago when there were multiple demands on my every hour. It's easier to concentrate on the here and now.

When I realize that I am limited only by the way I approach my life, then the half-empty part of my glass becomes full of possibilities. It waits for me to fill it to over-flowing with whatever I choose—a real blessing!

A Bike Ride To Remember

I went for an early morning ride on my bike. When I reached my destination, I turned around and thought to myself, "Now I am going back."

As I was riding along, another thought came to me: I never go back. I am always changed by my experiences when I get there. My life is always moving forward. There is nothing back there of much value to me, except a few lessons to be learned, and some memories. If I try to go back there, even for a moment, I risk losing the possibilities for this moment. When I think about that, I realize that to be fully open to all my opportunities, I must rid myself of guilt, anger, and resentment, because those feelings are all rooted in the past.

A little later I met a man with no legs propelling himself with his arms on a special wheeled vehicle. He was scooting along the road at a fast pace. He greeted me with a cheery smile and a vigorous "hello," and went on his way. I thought about that. Somewhere along the way, he seems to have discovered one doesn't need legs to enjoy the day. He appeared to be focusing on what he does have—two good arms, and the ability to be happy—and not on what he doesn't have—two good legs.

I think I sometimes focus on what I don't have—peace and quiet—and yet, I do have everything I need. I'm reminded that peace and quiet are within me, and not in my environment.

There is a lesson in all this. When I continually focus on the negative aspects of my life, I am unaware of all the opportunities available to me. When I use what I do have, there is virtually no limit to my choices.

Doing—Being

When I go to the beach in Florida I pick up shells that some creature has shed because it has outgrown the shell's confines. I think about that. The shedding of shells—perhaps that is why I am so drawn to summer weather. When I have shed most of my heavy clothes, I find it easier to shed some of life's encumbrances, those weights that drag me down and hamper my freedom, such as the endless task of keeping the house spotless and orderly—in case some one drops in unexpectedly. I would not want them to think—

This is a time in my life when I no longer need supports, things, organizations. I can live without approval—yes, even people. What I do need is freedom, space, time for meditation, for reading, writing, dreaming. I need to feed my spirit, to let my soul soar—to BE!

Doing has always come from compulsion, from pressure. One cannot live without doing, but I have arrived at a time when I wish for my doing to arise out of my sense of being. It will come from some inner prompting rather than from something outside myself. Perhaps that is the basic difference between the doing state and the being state. The former arises from external forces; the latter comes from one's innermost self. Doing often produces anxiety and dis-ease; Being always carries with it a sense of peace and well-being.

I must remember that I was a valued Being long before I could Do much of anything!

Is There Only One Way?

When I was a child in school I often knew the correct answer to a question without knowing why or how. In arithmetic, I could not solve the problems in the way they were described in the book, but my final answer was usually right. My teacher would not accept it, though, unless I could explain how I got it. I felt afraid and stupid when I could not explain a step-by-step process by which I arrived at some of my conclusions. In my child's mind, the teacher was the final authority, always right; therefore, I was wrong. After awhile, I gave up trying. I kept my answers to myself, figuring they were wrong anyway.

Eventually, I realized that I had to get through school. I learned to copy from others the logical steps to arrive at the answer I already knew. Since it was not my way of thinking, it didn't feel right, and only served to alienate me from myself. But the authorities seemed satisfied, and in due time I passed.

What a struggle I had in later years, to unlock my brain and let my intuition begin to work again for me!

I still don't know how or why I know many of the truths that come to me when I am relaxed and open to receiving. However, I am now less inclined to consider myself inadequate if I can't explain to your satisfaction some of the things I know. I am more likely to realize that we are not on the same wave-length. Neither is wrong—just different.

At last I do not have to give logical explanations in order to validate myself. What a relief!

We crucify the spirit over and over again when we teach little children that there is only one way to believe. The human mind can grow only when it is free to think and find its own meaning in what it discovers.

Who Cares?

"I don't care." An innocent sounding phrase, and yet, it is often packed with more emotional clutter than almost any other expression I know. It can generate anger, rejection, frustration, feelings of unworthiness, and most of all, the feeling of being unloved.

How so? Well, just listen to some of the ways we use that expression:

"Where do you want to eat?" "I don't care." But just take you to the wrong restaurant, and we'll see who cares.

"What do you want for lunch?" "I don't care." So I fix you a peanut butter and jelly sandwich. Right away I know that you really wanted shrimp salad and croissants.

"What should I wear?" "I don't care." So I wear jeans. Wrong again. The new blue outfit was on the roster for today.

And the list goes on and on. I really do care—and I know exactly what I want. After all these years, you should know, too. Right? But how could you know when I hide it so well deep inside me that even I often cannot find It?

What I really mean when I say, "I don't care," is that I don't want to take the responsibility for expressing my wishes. It might sound selfish; some one might not agree; I might not be able to have what I want, and then I would suffer. I might be wrong, and that would be awful.

"I don't care" also gets translated into "I'm not important," and that leads to alienation, a loss of self. I don't value myself enough to take the time to find out what I really want, or to think it is all right for me to care, and to express that caring, even at the risk of eliciting disapproval.

How sad to think of one's self as so unimportant, when in the eyes of the Eternal Spirit, even the smallest sparrow or the most insignificant rock is not ignored.

Lessons

I watched a little exchange between a mother and her small son, and I felt sad. He had apparently done something to displease her and she was very angry. She slapped him and then walked away from him. He was crying as if his heart would break, and maybe it did just a little. I would like to think this mother really cared about her son, and was intent on teaching him a lesson, but had not the understanding and insight necessary to be able to step into his shoes to see what was really going on, and how she might help him.

This little boy was learning, but I'm sure it was not the intended lesson, whatever that might have been in mother's head. What he was learning was that big people are mean and unloving when little people don't comply with what is expected of them, even when the expectations are unclear, unjust, or even unhealthy for the child. Is it any wonder we sometimes grow up to be uncertain, fearful, unkind, unjust, unloving?

I do not fault the mother for not knowing what she did not know, but I do have some questions about the relevance of education in a society that ignores the necessity of teaching human beings how to understand and get along with themselves and the world around them, including other humans.

Schools are really mixed up. We spend a lot of time teaching children how to read, and then don't trust them to go to books to find out what they need to know. We try to stuff it all into their heads. Meanwhile, what isn't in books, but can only be learned through direct, positive experience, is left to the individual to learn by chance. Many never do.

Enemies

What is an enemy? As a child, I dream up all kinds of enemies. The dark is my enemy, dragons and witches. Sometimes the forest or the jungle, or a big city, or the super-market, if I lose sight of Mom.

As I get older, my enemies become more real, or so I tell myself. The big bully down the block; school can become my enemy if there are demands made on me that are either unpleasant or seemingly impossible to satisfy. Big people who have power over little people can also be enemies.

When I become an adult, my real enemies take form—people who are different, people who want the same thing I want and thwart my effort to get it. Whole countries become an enemy if they threaten my security, or my favored position in the world. A criminal who gets what he wants by jeopardizing the lives of others is an enemy. The weather is my enemy if it interferes with my plans or threatens my existence. Hunger, thirst, poverty, disease—all are enemies, and I am frightened by all of them.

When I am afraid, I do many things to try to protect myself from my enemy. Unhappily, in this state, what I choose to do does nothing to alter the feared conditions. I only succeed in deluding myself into believing that I have made myself more secure, when, in fact, I have only made my "enemy" view me as the enemy, and that is when the real conflict begins.

If I were to stand on a mental mountain-top, even for a moment, and look down on me, and the scene which I have created, I would see there is really only one enemy that is real—myself, and my own fear.

Overcoming Adversity

The past has been a powerful influence in my life. It has often dictated how I did things, how I related to others and the world around me. I have felt handicapped because I couldn't get rid of old feelings of guilt and inadequacy. It seemed as though I would always have to be this way, and I blamed my parents for the part they played in creating my handicap.

One day, recently, I looked at a pine tree in my yard. Though it has been there as long as I can remember, I suddenly saw it anew. This tree did not grow straight and tall as most trees do. Long ago, when it was very small, something happened to permanently bend the trunk at a ninety-degree angle. The event must have been traumatic because the tree was never able to right itself. But that tree did not stop gowing. Though it could not get rid of the "bend," it continued to fulfill its destiny—it made another ninety-degree turn so it could grow toward the light, spread its branches, and drop its seeds, in order that other trees might sprout and grow straight and tall.

In the course of bringing up four children, I have repeated many old patterns of behavior, caused some "bends" to occur. But I have also discovered that the power of the past can be diminished if I choose a different way of being in the now. It is never too late to make changes. My tree is a powerful lesson in overcoming adversity.

I no longer need to feel guilty and inadequate for being human; and I can set an example in forgiveness for my children by forgiving my parents for the mistakes they made.

How marvelous to discover that some cycles can be discontinued!

Connections

This morning I open my eyes and find myself in that in-between state of half-asleep and half-awake. I suddenly feel as though I am walking in a wide, open space, with white mist floating around me. My footsteps echo. It is not a bad feeling, and I'm acutely aware that I am alone. I fear that no one will be around, and yet, I am not afraid, just wondering. Will I be connected? Or am I destined to be out there, always alone?

For a long time I have felt that God is not a person—that there is a life force which is not just apart from me, but also within me. And here is Vincent Stuart, in Changing Mind, saying:

> "Our raison d'etre lies within us by reason of there being a self-existing higher authority, sometimes called "God," not a figure of flesh and blood as presented by theologians, but our own inner highest state, which contains our spiritual forces."

If there is a connectedness in all of life, if all knowing is available to every living being, then it is not so strange that Stuart and I would be thinking the same thoughts. Our knowing comes from the same source. His ability to understand and describe that knowing may be more sophisticated than mine, but that does not make my knowing less important, or valid, or real.

Perhaps this is why, in the midst of aloneness, I do not feel lonely. This is when I am acutely aware of the connectedness of all living things.

Perhaps, also, this is why I feel so peaceful in natural surroundings. When all the noise created by my ego self, and that of all others, is silenced, then I can be aware that I am a part of a grand symphony creating the music of the inner life—where the Eternal Spirit resides, and is so real, so close, so obvious!

If I Could—

If I could go back sixty years and talk to the child I was, what would I say to her? Would I tell her not to do some things she chose to do? Would it help if I tried to reassure her that she would survive her pain, anxiety and uncertainty? I wonder if she would listen if I told her she would learn from the choices she made. If I pushed her to work harder, learn faster, would I be happier today?

Do you think I would be smart enough to thank her for all the agony and, yes, even the ecstasy she experienced in order to grow and develop?

I'm not perfect, nor am I finished yet with this life, but I am happy and feel peaceful most of the time. If I have any regrets about things done, or left undone, I must remember that everything that young woman did or experienced brought me to this juncture in my life. If I like it—and I do—then I will be eternally grateful to her, and the Spirit that guided her, for everything she ever did.

Alone?

Sometimes, when my ego self is in command, I feel alone, insignificant—unnoticed and unknown—in a vast, uncaring, universal sea. Like the minuscule shells on the ocean shore, I flop around in the changing tide, searching for a foothold to make me secure. But I am not alone. Others are out there, some just riding the waves, willing to be cast about by a force not their own; perhaps not even realizing that they have the power within to decide. A few are sure about where they want to go, no matter what the circumstances, and will resist whatever stands in their way. I can choose how it will be for me.

I think about those tiny shells, so perfect in every detail, almost too small to see. But I found them as I walked along the beach, even without being focused on the search. How much more powerful is the eye of the Divine Presence that seeks us out in remote corners to remind us that we are all a part of a universal plan, each one as worthy as the next.

I am not unnoticed after all.

2002

If your mind isn't clouded by unnecessary things,
This is the best season of your life.

Wu—Men

Delay

The days grow longer. The sun heats up. Spring arrives. Memorial Day weekend has come and gone, and here I am—still on Sanibel.

Once again, one of life's little glitches has conspired to keep me here and place me in the temporary role of caregiver. My husband, who remains loyal to his own specialty, has had re-constructive surgery on a thirteen-year-old hip prosthesis, and is now hobbling around on a walker—soon to graduate to a cane.

Stories of illness and death of long-time friends have begun to turn up in my mailbox, and I am forced into the realization of something I have known all along—physical life on this planet is fragile and tempo-rary. How blessed I am to be able to function in the role of caregiver! And how grateful we both are to have so many caring friends to lend a helping hand.

Though I miss the beginnings of spring weather at the river, my family tells me that winter has been reluctant to give up. The daffodils in my yard were, for a long time, too frozen to wither and fall over dead.

In a few short days we will begin the trek, in stages, to the north country. We are ready to exchange ninety-degree heat and round-the-clock air conditioning for long pants, jackets, fresh, crisp air and a cozy fire on the hearth.

My river continues its relentless flow to the sea and awaits my arrival.

Surface

Sun sparkles on the water like hundreds of clear crystal beads. The river in its relentless flow to the sea seems not to notice what happens on its surface. It allows the sun to play on it, but will not be delayed. It journeys on.

Some days the rain pelts down and the wind whips the water into powerful waves that may cause the river to appear as though it has changed direction, but it refuses to be distracted. It continues northward.

No external events or transient conditions raise any question about its final destination.

There is a lesson in this for me.

I sometimes let the trivia of everyday living seep into the core of my being and confuse me about the authenticity of my soul's journey. I begin to wonder where I am going, and raise the question: "Is it all right for me to follow my destiny, regardless of what happens on the surface of my life?"

These ruminations sap my energy and steal hours from my days. I don't like that. I am giving up valuable time that I can never get back.

Like the river with its singular intent, perhaps I, too, can grant the surface events of my life only their just due, and allow Creator to direct me back to the path I am intended to travel.

A Musing

On this day of clouds, wind and threatening rain, I will draw the shades early to shut out the cold gloom of early evening.

A few crackers and a glass of sherry lift my spirits as I go about preparing the evening meal.

After the demands of an eventful day, it is good to share a quiet dinner for two.

Blessings of joy and heightened sensitivity, like Sandborn's fog, creep in unannounced and unnoticed until a warm glow begins to spread into the deepest part of my being, and I am filled with awareness. I am in good health, my partner in life is doing well after unpleasant surgery. My family prospers and are eager for our company.

I lift my glass in celebration.

A Morning Musing

One morning this past spring, while still on Sanibel, I rode my bike to the beach and walked to the water's edge. The sea was placid. Gentle waves lapped the shore with a rhythmic swish, calming my restless spirit. Few people were out that early. Ibis, plovers, sandpipers and a lone snowy egret poked about for their breakfast, undisturbed. Pelicans floated on the water and gulls screamed overhead.

As I walked along in silence, I found it almost impossible to bridge the gap between such benign beauty and the other parts of the world where people grieve for loved ones lost in the tragedy of violence, where bombs fall on a fractured land, and children scrounge through garbage for whatever they can find to keep them alive.

I pondered the contrast and wondered how I could feel so peaceful, so secure within myself, so optimistic about the future in such an uncertain world. Is it all right to be happy while others mourn?

As I continued to walk, the answers came to me from somewhere deep inside. I cannot change the world, nor can I change other people. But perhaps I can make a difference in my limited space by contributing a portion of my resources, my time, my love and concern wherever I see a need.

Now, as I sit writing at my desk, I cherish the gift of this morning. I will pause for a moment of gratitude for all my blessings, and offer up a prayer for all those who have never known peace and plenty.

Lessons

A few years ago I had surgery on my ailing foot. My experience with pain and confinement was different from reading about it, hearing about it, or even observing it in others. I discovered a growing sense of empathy and compassion for all living things faced with some kind of disability.

Some time later I watched a squirrel dragging one useless hind leg across the front yard, gathering acorns for his winter supply of food. He stopped every now and then to lick the dangling foot, as if to ease the pain, then resolutely continued his search for food. With cheeks full of nuts he started up a nearby tree, no doubt headed for his home high in a nook of one of the gnarled branches. The going was rough with only one hind leg for pushing, but he persisted and made progress.

As I watched that squirrel, I marveled at his determination, and realized that here was a lesson for me. He was not sitting in some corner crying out at the injustice of it all, demanding that someone else attend to his needs. He had a problem, and all his energies seemed directed toward figuring out how to do what was important to him.

There were times during my recovery when I wanted to lash out at those helpful souls around me for not being available to wait on me at the very moment when I needed something. I wanted to scream at imagined injustice when my pillow was in the other room instead on the footrest where I needed it. My frustration knew no bounds.

Then I remembered the squirrel. I really didn't need a lot of help. I could use my walker to do some of my own errands. It just took a little longer and required more effort.

My foot healed and I was whole again. I doubt the squirrel was as fortunate.

The Courage To Wear Purple

When I was a child in school, practicing the "Palmer Method" of writing was an essential part of our every-day lessons. One exercise in particular, which caused me great difficulty, was filling the page with slanting up and down lines drawn close together, using a full arm motion. The goal was to get across the page keeping my lines confined within the boundaries of the horizontal lines on the paper. I never could do this.

My natural self was inclined to be spirited, adventuresome and a little bit wild, not wanting to be confined within boundaries prescribed by anyone else. As a result, I always ended up having to erase those parts where I "over-stepped" in order to gain approval. It didn't work. The teacher inevitably discovered my erasures and discredited me for my deception. That meant I had to work even harder to suppress my wandering instincts. Since I am, by nature, somewhat compulsive and perfectionist, over the years I succeeded in erasing those free-wheeling, spontaneous, and "different" parts of my being. I became alienated from important parts of my self. I learned to do my own discrediting.

How different it is in nature. The "standing people," a Native American expression for the trees in the forest, do not have unrealistic expectations for members of their own species. There always seems to be room for unusual configurations, the free unfettered growth of some individuals. There is a benign acceptance and ready accommodation of all sorts of deviations from the norm.

Who defines the norm, anyway? Who cares?

As I wander through the woods, I'm glad I can learn from those trees. It's nice to be able to review perceptions of self, constructed in the past, and release those which constrict and, or, no longer fit.

It's OK to wear a bit of purple!

The Move

Several years ago, while living in a small house on Sanibel, we decided that our living space was too small to comfortably accommodate visiting family members. The children had grown—we could no longer fit them into a corner. Jason wanted to sleep in a "real bed."

The move went without a hitch—until the first morning:

I woke up in a strange new house this morning. Help! I'm confused. I bumped my nose on a sliding glass door when I attempted to go to the bathroom in the middle of the night. I'm moving cautiously now as I wend my way to the "necessary room," a title our son coined when he was little.

Where is the light switch? Which towel is mine? And my hairbrush—it's not in its usual drawer. In fact, the drawer has moved to a different place.

How will I ever get dressed? When I open the bottom drawer where my shorts should be, all I find are shirts.

Stop! I want to go back to what was familiar. I loved that place. Why did I leave?

I know why I moved. I needed more space. In order to get that, I had to give up the old—the familiar—and stretch toward the new.

Life is full of endings and beginnings. Infancy gives way to childhood, which leads to adolescence, and then to adulthood. I can only imagine what it would be like to hang onto and carry around with me all those earlier stages. It would be like trying to grow with a brick on my head. My focus would be on my headache instead of my potential for growth.

If I concentrate on developing a new routine better suited to the rooms, drawers and cupboards in this house, I will then be free to enjoy its expanded view of the lake, and the lighter, more spacious place in which to live and entertain my friends and my family.

I'm glad I stretched!

Knowing?

When I look at a person I think I know, I see only my memory of that person—what he did yesterday—and what he usually does—what he has always done as far back as I can remember. I see my expectations of what that person will do—how he will react to me, and, by remembering, I will not allow him to escape his own history. I fashion my behavior to match what I expect of him.

In this way I create not only my own life, but his responses to me as well. I am the inventor of most of what happens to me.

However, If I can truly "forget" that person, I can see him anew each time we come in contact. I am free then, to create something new—never experienced before. I can become a different person by creating a whole new set of circumstances with this person whom I respect as someone entirely new to me. I can live a new life. Perhaps I can truly "know" this person—and myself, in the process.

But it seems risky, because he is doing the same thing. He remembers me, and expects me to react in certain ways, and he fashions his own behavior to match those expectations.

If I change, my behavior will seem strange to him and he may react with fear and anger. I'm afraid of that. So, I will continue in old patterns of behavior, based on memory, in order to prevent this reaction. Of course, that does not work, it only generates more of the same—and the cycle continues.

How nice to discover that it is never too late to discard those old patterns, take the risk of creating a whole different scenario, and start each new day as an adventure into the unknown. It's still exciting to grow!

Present Moments

Last night I sat on the porch with my friend. A brisk, warm breeze blew in our faces, gradually diminishing as we sat. The river began to calm after a day of choppy waves. The sun sat low in the western sky. We talked leisurely about everything and nothing, basking in a gentle, contented relationship—wholly occupied with the present moment.

Reflecting on that time of easy companionship, I am struck by the fact that the river is a great equalizer. My friend and I arose from disparate backgrounds with very different life experiences. Though most of our values are similar, we might find that we think quite differently about some issues—if we cared to explore them. But it doesn't matter. We are bound together by a shared love of this great river and its environs, and we try to make the most of our brief months together. It seems enough to focus on the things we have in common, and important to allow each other the freedom to live according to what is right for each.

As the sun began to set, I returned next door to my home to prepare our evening meal. I felt relaxed and rested, with a glimpse of how wondrous life would be if I could spend my days fully alive in my present moments. I could allow the past to fade into the background, and be disinclined to ruminate about what the future might hold.

Threads

The thread of life seems so fragile. It can be broken at any moment—an accident—an act of violence—a sudden unexpected illness.

I wake up in the morning and all seems serene. Before nightfall the winds of change turn the world upside down and I wonder why the flowers have the nerve to continue blooming. How do I carry on with my normal daily activities in the face of terrible headline news, the death of a close friend, or even an illness of someone close to me?

Once again I look to nature to help me find answers. I walk through the woods early in the morning. Spiders have been busy all night weaving their webs across my path. These threads, too, seem fragile, so fine that they are almost invisible, but as I walk along, I find it difficult to break them. They stretch and cling to my clothing. Meanwhile, the spider does not spend his time weeping and wailing over the broken or dislodged thread. He gets busy immediately, spinning and weaving to make repairs. By the time I return along that same path, the web, though different and perhaps a bit distorted, is intact and in good working order. His life goes on.

Perhaps it would be helpful to adopt some "spider" characteristics, and think about spinning my own web of connections with others who also face adversity.

Storm

Weeks have gone by with no significant rain. The flowers wilt unless watered daily—the grass has stopped growing and turned brown. After so much rain in the spring, we wish for a more even distribution. But we are not in control.

I notice the ducks and geese and birds don't seem to care about brown grass and wilted flowers. They have a casual approach to current weather conditions. All is well in the present moments. They refuse to be concerned about yesterday—or tomorrow. They only know enough to take action when the need arises to protect themselves and their young. What a marvelous way to live!

I'm remembering a time on Sanibel when I worried about the possible consequences of an approaching storm:

The wind blows hard. I watch black clouds roll over the tops of trees across the lake. Soon they engulf this whole end of the island. I wait in fear for the thunder, the lightning and rain.

Now, I cannot distinguish one cloud from another. The sky is dark gray.

All the birds have disappeared. Have they gone to a safe haven? Are they anxious as I am? The weather report warns of a severe thunderstorm, with possible tornadoes. Is my house a safe haven for me?

The clouds take shape—a series of fast-moving, boiling configurations race across the sky. They empty their moisture-laden contents in a fury onto the parched land.

There is no thunder as I had expected, no flashing light across the leaden sky—just a steady downpour of much-needed rain.

I relax a little, and open the sliding-glass door slightly, so I can hear the sound of rain falling on the lake.

Suddenly an osprey flies across the sky, whistling his high-pitched cry. Other birds appear. Is this a signal to me that the danger is past?

My fear was unfounded, and begins to dissipate as I listen to the sounds of nature reassuring me that this is not a storm to threaten my existence. Instead of worrying about what might happen, why can't I learn from the birds—forget the worry and focus only on being prepared to take flight if necessary.

Summer's End

The calendar tells me that Labor Day is just around the corner—so soon? Didn't I just arrive at my northern paradise? Does time really fly?

Schools will begin—the State Park will close—leaves will change color—morning dew will cover the lawn chairs. I can't ignore the signs.

My daughter, Melanie Pyke Hertzog was born in the month of July, and has spent most of her birthdays at the Thousand Islands. The river is in her blood. It seems fitting that I would share, in closing this season, her September experience:

"It is Autumn Equinox and we are blessed with a perfect day on the river. Summer lingers in emerald shades deep in the woods, but it is August no longer. The summer songbirds have departed. Punctuated against the sudden quiet are a few sounds—a high chitter of crickets, the earnest squeaking of chipmunks, chickadees calling—a warning cry from a migrating blue jay.

"The ground is strewn with multitudes of acorns which crunch underfoot. Bang! One tumbles through branches overhead and bounces off the beachfront deck.

"Everything is clear and sharp in the crisp fall air. The water at the beach is crystalline as from a spring, with ribbons of sunlight flickering across the sandy bottom. The water level has dropped so that shoals, normally submerged, now lie uncovered. The dock towers above the tumble of rocks around the supporting cribbs.

"At day's end, the sky is washed with color. A molten trail shimmering in the water leads my eyes into the fiery sunset. The light fades quickly and I shiver in the sudden evening chill. The rising harvest moon shines through the black tree-forms. Their fullness elicits memories of sitting on summer docks, imagining shapes of wolves and glaring witches looming into the starry universe.

"As I ascend the beachfront stairs, I know, without waiting to see, that throughout the night, the moon will light its sparkling path across the quiet river. In the pre-dawn hours it will slide, a spent orange disc, behind the formless horizon.

"When the sky has emptied, the world will stand hushed, motionless. It will be as a scratchboard—untouched—waiting for the Artist to begin the first strokes of light and color in the creation of a new day."

Shalom!

Who Speaks To Me?

Everywhere I go I get messages. Some are soft and subtle; some are loud and clear. My body speaks to me—my eyes, ears, nose, my heart, and my skin. When I am ill, even my hair tells me there is something wrong.

The sky tells me things. The wind whispers in my ear or shouts from the treetops. Birds tell me much if I will learn to read their language: from the tiniest chirping of a sparrow to the raucous screeching of the crow as he shouts out his warning to the rest of the animal kingdom. People tell me many things:. from the slightest lift of an eyebrow and a faint twitch of a facial muscle, to a clearly verbalized message.

But this does not account for all my knowing. How do I sometimes know who is calling me before I pick up the phone? Who reminds me of a long forgotten experience, a name, a place? What prompted me to pick up this special book to read a certain passage just when it would be most helpful to me? Where do insights come from?

Does knowing happen when my mind is open to the relatedness of all of life, and to the universal knowledge of the ages? How wonderful! What infinite possibilities!

There is a stirring deep within me that says:

"Let go of fear and mistrust. Have faith that the direction of your life proceeds in a way which is good for you and will not harm others. Relax and do not be afraid to trust. Take this day and live it as if you have pulled out all the stops on the organ and the music is flooding the earth—and there is peace, triumph.

Reach out and greet life with joy and love. You have a destiny. The Eternal Spirit speaks to you and through you. Listen, and this Spirit will guide you. You are not alone and you cannot go wrong."

I see all around me evidence of inhumanity to fellow travelers and to the world. But I also see the beauty, the grandeur, the nobility, the everlasting quality of the human spirit; and I know I have choices.

I can choose to be small, limited and mean, impoverished, helpless, hopeless; or I can listen to the symphony of the universe, the history of the ages, and know there is creative energy in the sun, the moon, the stars, the earth, in me and all humankind just waiting to be activated. God of the universe, Creative Mind, Supreme Intelligence speaks to me. I pray that I may listen and learn.

About the Author

Born in Springfield, Massachusetts in 1922, Vivian Pyke graduated from Syracuse University in 1943, and in1971 obtained a masters degree in Social Work.

She maintained a private practice as a Psychiatric Social Worker until retirement in 1987. With her husband, Dr. Charles Pyke, she now divides her time between the Thousand Islands in northern New York and Sanibel Island, Florida.

0-595-29242-9